TAKE YOUR BIKE

Family Rides in the Rochester Area

TAKE YOUR
BIKE

Family Rides in the Rochester Area

www.footprintpress.com

Footprint Press, Inc. publishes a variety of guidebooks to outdoor recreation. See a complete list and order form at the back of this book. We also publish a free Blog called *New York Outdoors.* To sign up, go to: http://newyorkoutdoors.wordpress.com

Trail Locations by Trail Number

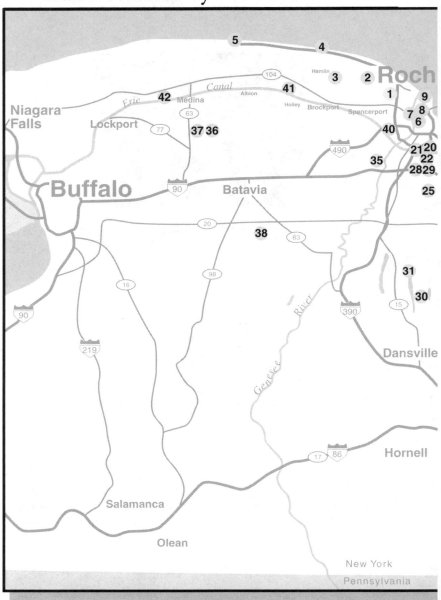

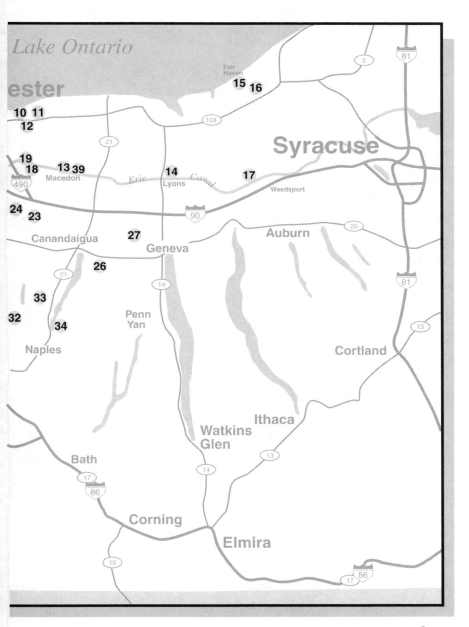

Lake Ontario

ester

Fair Haven

15 16

10 11
12

104

Syracuse

21

19
18 **13 39**
Macedon

Erie **14** Canal
Lyons

17

490

Weedsport

24 **23**

90

Canandaigua

27
Geneva

Auburn

20

81

26

21

14

33

32

34

Penn
Yan

81

13

Naples

Cortland

Ithaca

Watkins
Glen

Bath

13

17
86

14

Corning

Elmira

15

17 86
17

CONTENTS

Trail Development & Acknowledgments 9

Introduction 11

How to Use this Book 13

Legend 14

Map Legend 17

Directions 18

Guidelines 19

History of the Bicycle 20

Types of Bikes 23

Safety 25

Bicycling With Children 26

A Word About Dogs 27

Clothing and Equipment 28

Bike Racks 29

Rides Northwest of Rochester
1. Greece Interstate 390 Trail 32
2. Hilton Hojack Trail 37
3. Hamlin Hojack Trail 41
4. Hamlin Beach State Park 45
5. Lakeside Beach State Park 49

City Rides
6. Genesee Valley Park & Genesee Valley Greenway Loop . . .54
7. Genesee River - Downtown Loop Trail 61

Contents

8. Mount Hope Cemetery 68

9. North Genesee River Trail 73

Rides Northeast of Rochester

10. Webster - Hojack Trail 80

11. North Ponds Park Trail 84

12. Webster - Route 104 Trail 87

13. Historic Macedon Erie Canal Route 91

14. Canal Park Trailway 96

15. Fair Haven - Cato Trail (Cayuga County Trail) 101

16. Hannibal - Hojack Trail 107

17. Howland Island 110

Rides Southeast of Rochester

18. Perinton Hike-Bikeway 116

19. Western Hike-Bikeway to Thomas Creek Wetlands . . .121

20. Historic Erie Canal and Railroad Loop Trail 126

21. Electric Trolley Trail 131

22. Cartersville - Great Embankment Loop Trail 134

23. Auburn Trail 139

24. Victor - Lehigh Valley Trail 147

25. Mendon - Lehigh Valley Trail 150

26. Ontario Pathways Trail (Canandaigua to Stanley) 157

27. Ontario Pathways Trail (Stanley to Phelps) 163

Rides South of Rochester

28. Hansen Nature Center Trail 170

29. Royal Coach Trail 174

30. Canadice Lake Trail 178

31. Hemlock Lake & Big Oaks Trails 183

32. Harriet Hollister Spencer Memorial State Recreation Area .187

33. Stid Hill Multiple Use Area 192

34. Middlesex Valley Rail Trail 196

Rides Southwest of Rochester

35. Genesee Valley Greenway (Chili to Cuylerville) 202

36. Oak Orchard Wildlife Management Area 211

37. Iroquois National Wildlife Refuge and
Tonawanda Wildlife Management Area 216

38. Genesee County Park and Forest 221

Erie Canalway Trail 228

39. Erie Canalway Trail (Palmyra to Pittsford) 231

40. Erie Canalway Trail (Pittsford to Spencerport) 240

41. Erie Canalway Trail (Spencerport to Albion) 247

42. Erie Canalway Trail (Albion to Lockport) 254

Additional Resources 263

The Recycle Cycle Program 265

Guided Bike Tours 266

Definitions 268

Trails by Length 270

Loop Trails 273

Trails by Difficulty 274

Trails by Amenities 276

Word Index 277

About the Authors 282

Books Available from Footprint Press, Inc. 284

Bookhug Book Holder 286

Order Form 287

Trail Development & Acknowledgments

The greater Rochester area is a community blessed with civic leaders and private citizens who have preserved our heritage and built the trails described in this book for all of us to enjoy. Through the preservation of abandoned railroad corridors and the development of trails along major arteries, they're gradually building a network of trails that will someday crisscross our area. Each year, more miles are opened as the land is secured, brush is cleared, and bridges are built to span our many waterways.

Two major initiatives began in 2002 that bode well for our chances of having an interconnected system of trails in the near future. The Genesee Transportation Council conducted a study to identify and prioritize the building of trails and bridges to connect existing trails. (For details on this initiative see web site http://www.gtcmpo.org.) Also, a new organization called the Genesee Region Trails Coalition was formed. Its goal is to promote cooperation among private organizations and public agencies who are working on trails, greenways, open space, and linear parks in the Genesee Region to develop trails from a regional perspective, coordinate resources and promote the awareness and use of trails.

To local volunteer trail organizations, we owe a debt of gratitude. Without their hard work and dedication, we wouldn't have trails to ride or walk. We also thank the leaders of these groups for lending their support in the making of this book. These groups include:

Crescent Trail Association
Friends of Genesee Valley Greenway
Friends of Webster Trails
Hansen Nature Center
Macedon Trail Committee (Peter S. Henry)
The Mendon Foundation
Ontario Pathways (Kyle Gage)
Penfield Trails Committee (Jim Britt)
Rochester Bicycling Club (Todd Calvin)
Victor Hiking Trails

Likewise, it's foresight, planning, and action by our public officials that result in paths dedicated to us bicyclists and outdoors enthusiasts. Kudos and thanks go to:

Cayuga County Planning Board
City of Rochester, Bureau of Parks and Recreation (Jim Farr)
City of Rochester, Water and Lighting Bureau (Don Root)
Hamlin Beach State Park (James Slusarczyk)
Henrietta Parks Department (Bill Dykstra)
Lakeside Beach State Park (Thomas J. Rowland)
Monroe County Parks Department
New York State Canal Corporation
New York State Department of Environmental Conservation
Pittsford Parks and Recreation Department
Town of Greece
Town of Webster
Wayne County Planning Department
Webster Parks and Recreation Department

A special thanks to Karen Howe, the owner of Moondance Pet Boarding in Hamlin for directing us to the Hilton and Hamlin sections of the Hojack Trail. Now more people will be able to enjoy these beautiful stretches of trail.

Finally, thank you to Susan Domina. Her fine proofreading skills made this a much better book.

Introduction

If you walk into a bike shop in Rochester and ask where you can go bike riding and be safely off roads, you're likely to hear about the canal towpath, also known as the Erie Canalway Trail, but not much else. That trail is spectacular, and we include it in this book. But, many other options are available around Rochester; they're just a well kept secret. Well, the secret is out! This book is loaded with havens that you can retreat to for a short respite or a long adventure. Choose the length and type of terrain to fit the ability of the participants.

We enjoy bike riding very much. It makes us feel good, it's fun, it's healthy, and it's inexpensive — a great combination. But, we don't particularly like riding the narrow shoulder of a busy road as cars and trucks zip by within inches of our bikes. That's not relaxing, and it's certainly not fun. Biking doesn't have to be like that. Off-road alternatives exist that are much more conducive to a family outing or an invigorating adventure. You'll find them in this book.

The American Heart Association recommends 30 to 60 minutes of physical activity at least 3 to 4 times per week to maintain cardiovascular fitness. You're more likely to achieve this level if you pick activities that you enjoy and that are convenient. Biking is a perfect way to improve the fitness of your heart and lungs. It burns calories too. Here's a breakdown of approximate calorie use per hour for three weight categories:

Person's weight:	100 lb.	150 lb.	200 lb.	
bicycling 6 mph	160	240	312	calories burned per hour
bicycling 12 mph	270	410	534	calories burned per hour

You don't need a special (or expensive) bike to enjoy these trails. The only bike that isn't suited to an off-road venture is a road-racing bike. There are a few exceptions where rugged trails require a mountain bike but they are clearly labeled. See the section "Types of Bikes" for specifics on the types of bikes available. The important thing is to grab this guide, hop on your bike, and go for a ride.

And, why stop at bicycling? Many of the trails listed in this book are equally well-suited to hiking, cross-country skiing, bird watching,

11

rollerblading, running, and strolling. Enjoy them at various seasons and using various means of locomotion. Each visit can be a unique experience. CAUTION: If you venture onto the rural trails during the fall hunting season, be sure to wear blaze orange so that hunters can spot you easily.

Many of the trails in this book were built by and are maintained by volunteer or community groups. They all welcome new members, especially anyone who is willing to help with the work. We encourage everyone to join a trail group and benefit from the camaraderie and service to your community. Except for trails located in state parks, the trails listed in this book are free and open to the public. You do not need to be a member of the sponsoring group to enjoy the trails.

How To Use This Book

We have clustered the trails into six geographic groups, using downtown Rochester as the center dividing point:

Rides Northwest of Rochester
City Rides
Rides Northeast of Rochester
Rides Southeast of Rochester
Rides South of Rochester
Rides Southwest of Rochester
Erie Canalway Trail

The trails range in length from a short 1.2 miles to 97 miles. An index in the back of the book ranks the trails by length so that you can select ones to fit the endurance of your group. Some of the trails are loops, but most, because they are converted railroad beds, are not. When you retrace the route, the return trip can often look quite different from your new perspective, even though you're covering the same ground. Or, to add variety, there is always the option of riding one way on the trails and the other on the roads. Some of the trails can be joined to lengthen your ride. Or shorten the ride by turning back at any point along the route or parking a car at one of the alternative parking spots listed.

The riding times given are approximate and assume a moderate pace of 6 to 7 miles per hour. You may find that you travel faster or slower, so adjust the times accordingly. Also, adjust the times to include stops or breaks for resting, eating, observing nature, viewing historical artifacts, and the like. You can easily stretch a two-hour bike ride into an all-afternoon affair if you take time to enjoy the adventure along the way.

We listed some of the amenities you'll find as you travel. After all, when you work hard on a bike ride, you deserve a treat. (You'll quickly find as you read this book that we're ice cream lovers.) We also indicate bike shops that are located near the trails in case you require emergency repairs.

13

Legend

At the beginning of each trail listing, you'll find a map and a description with the following information:

Location: A general description of the town the trail is located in and the endpoints of the trail.

Parking: Where to park to follow the trail as described in the Trail Directions.

Alternative Parking: Other parking locations with access to the trail. Use these if you want to shorten your ride by starting or stopping at a spot other than the designated endpoints.

Riding Time: The approximate time that it will take to bike the trail one way at a moderate pace of 6 to 7 miles per hour, adjusted for the difficulty of the terrain. Add to this "riding time," the amount of time you stop for breaks, sightseeing, or other fun adventures to arrive at the total time needed for any particular outing.

Length: The distance from start to finish. The mileage is labeled as a loop, one-way, or round trip.

Difficulty: A ranking of the amount of elevation change and surface conditions you can expect. Each trail is rated as easy, moderate, or difficult.

Easy = Generally flat, a paved or hard-packed riding surface.

Moderate = Could be hilly or a softer riding surface, so you'll pump those pedals harder.

Difficult = Quite hilly or a rough trail. You'll get an aerobic workout for sure.

Surface: The materials that make up the surface for the majority of the trail.

Trail Markings: Markings used to designate the trails in this book vary widely. Some trails are not marked at all but are cleared or worn paths which you can easily follow. As long as there aren't many intersecting, unmarked paths, you shouldn't lose your way. Other trails are well marked with either signs, blazes, or markers and sometimes a combination of all three. Trail markings are established by the official group that maintains the trail.

Signs - wooden or metal signs with instructions in words or pictures.

Blazes - painted markings on trees showing where the trail goes. Many blazes are rectangular and placed at eye level. Colors may be used to denote different trails. If a tree has twin blazes beside or on top of one another, you should proceed cautiously because the trail either turns or another trail intersects.

Markers - small plastic or metal geometric shapes (square, round, triangular) nailed to trees at eye level to show where the trail goes. They also may be colored to denote different trails.

Uses: Each trail has a series of icons depicting the activity or activities allowed on the trail. These include:

Hiking   Bicycling   Wheelchairs   Rollerblading

Jogging   Horseback riding   Snow-mobiling   Cross-country skiing

Contact: The address and phone number of the organization to contact if you would like additional information or if you have any questions not answered in this book.

———————	Major Road	★	Trail Location
———————	Secondary Road		Water
+++++++++	Railroad	~	River or Creek
··············	Power Lines		Park Boundary
▥	Boardwalk		
<	Canal Lock		Marsh
⦚	Barrier	**P**	Parking
⤬	Bridge	155	County Route
⌂	Lean-to or Shelter	(104)	State Route
■	Building	(90)	Interstate Route
⑰	Trail Post Number	•••••	Trail
✈	Airport	::::::	Double Track Trail
		▪▪▪▪▪	Other Trail
		– – – –	Hiking Trail Only

Trail Blaze Colors:

Blue - Ⓑ	Orange - Ⓞ	White - Ⓦ
Brown - ⒝ⓡ	Purple - Ⓟ	Yellow - Ⓨ
Green - Ⓖ	Red - Ⓡ	
Grey - ⒢ⓨ	Violet - Ⓥ	

17

Directions

In the directions we often tell you to turn left or right. To avoid confusion in some instances we have noted a compass direction in parentheses according to the following:

(N) = north
(S) = south
(E) = east
(W) = west

Some trails have "Y" or "T" junctions. A "Y" junction indicates one path that turns into two paths. The direction we give is either bear left or bear right. A "T" junction is one path that ends at another. The direction is turn left or turn right.

Guidelines

Any adventure in the outdoors can be inherently dangerous. It's important to watch where you are going and keep an eye on children. Some of these trails are on private property where permission is benevolently granted by the landowners. Please respect the landowners and their property. Follow all regulations posted on signs and stay on the trails. Our behavior today will determine how many of these wonderful trails remain for future generations to enjoy.

Follow "no-trace" ethics whenever you venture outdoors. "No-trace" ethics means that the only thing left behind as evidence of your passing are your footprints or tireprints. Carry out all trash you carry in. Do not litter. In fact, carry a plastic bag with you and pick up any litter you happen upon along the way. The trails included in this book are intended for day trips. Please, no camping or fires except where specifically allowed such as at some campsites along the Erie Canalway Trail. (See the index under camping.)

As the trails age and paths become worn, trail work groups sometimes reroute the trails. This helps control erosion and allows vegetation to return. It also means that if a sign or marker doesn't appear as it is described in the book, it's probably due to trail improvement.

Remember:

Take only pictures, leave only prints.

Please do not pick anything.

History of the Bicycle

For much of man's history on earth, he had two choices for getting around, either on foot or on the back of an animal (such as horses, mules, and wooly mammoths). Bicycles were developed to add another transportation option that multiplied human efficiency by a factor of approximately five. But the history of bicycles is very fuzzy. Sources often disagree as to the names of the inventors and the dates of their inventions. Leonardo DaVinci sketched a facsimile of the modern bicycle in 1490. It was way ahead of its time and, as far as we know, never left the drawing board. Around 1790 a French crafts-

DaVinci's sketch

man named de Sivrac developed a "Celerifere" running machine, which had two in-line wheels connected by a beam. The rider straddled the beam and propelled the Celerifere by pushing his feet on the ground, scooter fashion.

Celerifere

In 1817 German Baron Karl von Drais added steering. Several versions appeared around France and England by the early 1800s. As a replacement for the horse, these "hobby horses" became a short-lived craze. The roads of the time were too rutted to allow for efficient wheeled transport.

Scottish blacksmith Kirkpatrick MacMillan developed a rear-drive bike in 1839 using a treadle and rod for the rear drive mechanism. But, he lived in the Northern British Isles where people and ideas traveled slowly, so his invention didn't spread.

R.W. Thompson patented a pneumatic tube in 1845. Prior to this invention, bikes had metal wheels.

The French anointed Ernest Michaux "father of the bicycle," as he and his brother Pierre added cranks and pedals. Their Velocipede started a bicycle boom. The larger front wheel made it faster but less stable. The war of 1812 brought an end to the French bicycle boom.

Velocipede

British engineers were next to pick up the design and improve upon it by adding ball bearings, pneumatic (Dunlop) tires, wire-spoked wheels, chain drive, variable gears, and cable controls. Over a twenty-year span, the British brought the bicycle to its present form, thanks mainly to James Starley of the Coventry Sewing Machine Company. In 1885 the Starley Rover safety bike was born, returning wheels to a reasonable size and improving the bike's stability.

Safety Bicycle

The bicyling craze began in Rochester around 1880. After practicing in a rented hall, nine brave men hit the streets of Rochester on bicycles. Their endeavors led to formations of the Rochester Bicycling Club, cycling schools, bicycle races, and in 1899, a bicycle festival and parade which attracted a large crowd.

Rochester's first bike path was opened in Charlotte, and the Sidepath Association sold usage licenses for $0.25 per year. By 1901 Monroe County had 125 miles of cinder paths for bicycling.

In the early days, women's dress (corsets, pointed shoes, and voluminous skirts) limited their participation in this new sport. And, newspapers of the day railed against the "sorcers" or bicycle speedsters.

Our first famous bicyclist was Rochester native Nick Kaufman, who gathered a chestful of medals on a world tour as a trick cyclist.

A more recent famous Rochester area person in the bike world is Georgena Terry of Macedon. In 1985 Georgena, a mechanical engineer by day and bike builder by night, listened to female friends complain of back, shoulder and neck pain, and recognized the problems inherent in modern diamond-style bicycle frames. Her revolutionary solution was the Terry Bicycle. She built the front wheel smaller than the back wheel and changed the fork angle to help women sit upright and more comfortably. Today, this woman-owned company designs and produces bicycles made for womens" proportions. They are the only mass distributors of bicycles for women in this country. They also make accompanying women's gear from cycle shorts to gloves. Check out their web site at www.terrybicycles.com.

Bicycling has a colorful and inventive history. To fully appreciate it and to see examples of every variety of bicycle made in the USA, visit the Pedaling History Museum near Buffalo (3943 North Buffalo Road, Orchard Park, NY 14127-1841, (716) 662-3853, www.pedalinghistory.com).

Types of Bikes

If you've shopped for a bicycle within the last ten years or so, you know that the choice can be overwhelming. So many types of bikes are available with unfamiliar names like hybrid, derailleur, cruisers, mountain bikes, BMX, adult ballooners, and coaster-brake bikes. Gear speeds range from 1 to 21 speeds. To ride the trails listed in this book, you don't have to be an expert on bikes or have a specific type of bike. Many of the bikes housed in garages today (and found often at garage sales) are quire suitable on these trails. Let's review the major groups:

10-Speed Bikes

Derailleur bikes are commonly called 10-speed bikes, but they come in 5, 6, 10, 12, 15, or 20 speeds. The derailleur, a French word meaning "to derail," either lifts or pushes the chain from one gear to the next. These bikes are generally lightweight with drop handlebars, hand brakes, no fenders, a narrow saddle, and high pressure tires. Designed to be racing bikes and long-distance road bikes, their popularity boomed in the 1970s. Derailleur bikes can be used on any of the paved trails in this book; they are not suited to the non-paved trails.

Single-Speed, Coaster-Brake Bikes

Baby boomers like us have grown up with these bikes. They are heavy bikes with low-pressure balloon tires, wide upright handlebars, a large

padded seat, and as the name implies, only one speed.   Braking is accomplished by backpedaling. Tough, sturdy work-horses, these bikes last a long time and can take a pounding on the trails listed in this book. Because of the single speed, you may occasionally find yourself walking up a hill. (But we do that anyway even with our 15-speed bikes!)

Cruisers or Adult Ballooners

Internal-hub-geared bikes or cruisers have many features in common
 with the single-speed, coaster-brake
bikes except that they do have gear
shifting. The shifting mechanism is
contained inside the rear hub and is
activated by hand brakes and cables
from the handlebars. They come in 2,
3, or 5 speeds. The term "ballooners"
derives from their fat, low-pressure tires. They make excellent trail bikes.

Comfort Bikes

As the name implies, these are built for comfort with upright seating,
wide seats, and wide tires. They're designed for short distance riding.

BMX Bikes

BMX is an abbreviation for Bicycle
Moto-Cross. These tough bikes are
mini-ballooners with fat tires originally
designed for trick riding both on and
off road.

Mountain Bikes

Also called all-terrain bikes (ATB), mountain bikes became the rage of
the 1990s. They offer the functionality of a 10-speed bike with the dura-
 bility of a cruiser. Mountain bikes typi-
cally have flat handlebars; heavy-duty
brake levers; indexed, thumb-shift
levers; wide, knobby tires; heavy-duty
rims; and reinforced frames. They're
designed to be light weight and strong,
as an all-terrain vehicle. Mountain bikes are available in 10, 15, 18, and
21 speeds.

Hybrid Bikes

A bike that can run on trails or roads with flat handlebars and tires
mid-way between road bike thinness and mountain bike fatness.

Safety

Regardless of age, everyone who hops on a bike should wear an approved, protective helmet. It's the law in New York State for anyone under the age of 14. Wearing a bicycle helmet significantly reduces the chances of a serious brain injury if you fall off of your bike. Unfortunately, every year nearly 50,000 bicyclists suffer serious head injuries. Many never fully recover, and often the injuries are fatal. Why take the risk when prevention is so simple?

It's important that the helmet fits properly. It should sit level, cover your forehead, and not slide backward. Helmets come in many sizes; select one that feels comfortable and doesn't pinch. Then, use the sizing pads supplied with the helmet for "fine tuning" to achieve a snug fit. Finally, adjust the straps so that they are snug but not pinching. Now you're ready for an enjoyable and safe ride.

Courteous biking can help ensure that trails stay open for bikers. When you're around others, ride to the right in single file. Always signal before passing. It's easy for a bicycle to quickly sneak up on a pedestrian or slower biker and startle them. To avoid this, call out as you approach someone. A simple "on your left" alerts the person to your presence and lets them know which side you're approaching from. When you stop, pull off to the side of the path. Be conscious not to impede the progress of others. Stay on the trails. Do not create or use shortcuts, as they can result in added erosion to the area.

Bicycling with Children

Children love the excitement of bike riding. Add to that new surroundings to explore, and you're sure to have a fun-filled adventure. Ensure a pleasant trip with these simple tips. Plan to take frequent breaks. Carry lots of water and some snacks. Play a game along the way. Read ahead in this guide and assign your child the task of finding the next area of interest. Let your child pick the next break spot. Take time to stop, point out, and discuss things you find on the trail, such as beaver dams, animal tracks, and flowers.

You may have noticed that it's hard to find helmets small enough for an infant. There's a good reason for that. Infants under 12 months of age should not ride in a bicycle child seat, trailer, sidecar, or any other carrier. The fact is that babies are so susceptible to brain injuries that the risks outweigh the rewards. More than a third of the injuries to babies in carriers occur when the bicycle falls over while standing still. So, please wait until your child is a year old before taking him or her along on this enjoyable sport.

Once your child passes the one-year mark, you can begin using a child seat that mounts on the bike's rear wheel or a child trailer that gets pulled behind your bike. Make sure that the child is wearing an approved helmet and is securely but comfortably belted. The bicycle should have spoke protectors to assure that the child's feet stay out of harms way. The child seat should be high enough to support the child's head. Remember, when transporting a child in a child seat or trailer, your bicycle will require a longer breaking distance, will be less maneuverable, and will swerve if the child shifts suddenly.

A Word about Dogs

Outings with dogs can be fun with their keen sense of smell and different perspective on the world. Many times they find things that we would have passed without noticing. They're inquisitive about everything and make excellent companions. But to ensure that your "outing companion" enjoys the time outside, you must control your dog. Dogs are required to be leashed on most maintained public trails. The reasons are numerous, but the top ones are to protect dogs, to protect other hikers and bikers, and to ensure that your pet doesn't chase wildlife. Good dog manners go a long way toward creating goodwill and improving tolerance to their presence.

Most of the trails listed in this book welcome dogs. The only trails which prohibit dogs are:

8. Mount Hope Cemetery
28. Hansen Nature Center Trail

Clothing and Equipment

You don't need much more than a sturdy bicycle and a helmet to enjoy these trails. But here are some tips about clothing to wear and miscellaneous equipment to bring along. Shoes that tie or buckle are best; slip-on shoes could slip off unless they fit snugly. Sandals are not recommended. Sneakers are a good choice.

Dress in layers so that you can peel down as your heart rate rises during the trip. You'll probably have to put the layers back on when you stop for a break. We find it convenient to have a handle-bar bag on the front of our bikes for discarded clothing and other items.

The one accessory that's mandatory is a bottle of water. It's easy to put a bottle holder on your bike or toss a water bottle in a handle-bar bag. Keeping hydrated is important even on a short trip.

Other handy things to have are an energy snack, a tire patch kit and pump, a first-aid kit, a bike lock, insect repellent, sunscreen, a hat, a raincoat, and this guidebook. In summer, if you're biking near water (such as North Ponds Park, Hamlin Beach State Park, or Cayuga County Trail), don't forget your swimsuit and towel.

Bike Racks

The first challenge in being able to enjoy the trails listed in this book is getting your bicycle to the trailheads. This often requires some sort of bike rack. Bike racks come in many varieties and many prices. You can spend well over $200 or pick up one inexpensively at a garage sale. Before you head out shopping, think about the following questions to help you select a rack to fit your needs.

1. What vehicle will be used to reach the trailheads?
2. How many bikes will you need to transport?
3. Do the bikes all have quick-release front wheels?
4. Are any of the bikes an unusual size or shape (for example a small child's bike)?
5. Who will load the bicycles on the rack? Are they strong enough to lift the bicycles to the roof?
6. Will you need the extra security of a lockable bike rack?
7. Will the rack be specifically for bikes or do you also need to carry skis or other sports equipment?
8. How often are you likely to use the rack?
9. How much do you want to spend?

No rack is ideal for all vehicles and users. The trade offs you make will depend on your situation. For instance, if you plan to use the rack infrequently, you may be willing to trade some ease-of-use for a lower price. Here's some of the variety you'll find as you shop:

• Roof racks attach to the top of a vehicle. It's important to know if your vehicle has gutters or not. Roof racks can be noisy from wind resistance. They require someone with strength to hoist the bicycles to the roof. You have to be careful not to forget that the bicycles are up there and drive into a garage. (We know this from experience!) With some roof racks, you can't open your vehicle's sun roof, however, they do allow full access to your trunk.

• Rear racks mount on the back of a vehicle with brackets and straps. They can scratch paint and can be hard to attach. Most limit your access to the trunk, but they are generally inexpensive, and you can load bikes quite easily.

- Hitch racks mount on the rear of a vehicle but use a trailer hitch as their main point of attachment. They're less likely to scratch your vehicle but are more expensive.
- Sport trailers are good for carrying many bicycles, but remember that you'll pay extra if you drive on a toll road. These trailers obviously require more storage space.

Rides Northwest of Rochester

Greece Interstate 390 Trail

1.

Greece Interstate 390 Trail

Location: Parallel to Interstate 390 from Ridge Road West (Route 104) to the Lake Ontario State Parkway, Greece, Monroe County

Parking: Greece Odyssey School parking lot on Hoover Drive, just south of the Olive Garden Restaurant on Ridge Road West (Route 104)

Alternative Parking: Greece Olympia School, Maiden Lane, Greece

Basil A. Marella Park, English Road, Greece (across from Parkland School)

Riding Time: 1.5 hours round trip

Length: 10.4 miles round trip

Difficulty: Easy, small rolling hills

Surface: Paved

Trail Markings: Green-and-white metal signs on posts showing a biker above the numbers 390

Uses: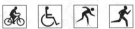

Facilities: Many restaurants are near the start of the trail on West Ridge Road.

Greece Odyssey School has a playground.

Basil A. Marella Park has hiking trails, playground, a WorldTrail® exercise trail, a disc golf course, restrooms, fields for baseball, volleyball, and soccer, and tennis courts.

Dogs: OK on leash

Admission: Free

Contact: Town of Greece, Department of Human Services 500 Maiden Lane, Rochester, NY 14616 (585) 663-0200

33

The pedestrian and bicycle bridge across busy Route 104.

Enjoying the easy-riding, paved path of the Greece Interstate 390 Trail.

This bike path slices through the town of Greece giving the cyclist a sample of its diversity from busy Ridge Road, to suburban backyards, to deep woods, and fields. On the way you may see rabbits, great blue herons, turtles, and ducks, not to mention the usual birds, squirrels, and chipmunks. The ride north is an easy pedal, but save some energy. Your return will be slightly uphill.

This path is well marked. In addition to metal signs reading "390 biking" on posts, at each crossing you'll see the silhouette of a biker painted on the asphalt. We jokingly call this marking "the roadkill biker."

If you haven't expended enough energy by the time you complete this trek, the Greece Odyssey School has a WorldTrail® Fitness Course that you can try while your kids romp in the playground. Or, if you've worked up a monumental hunger, Applebee's, Olive Garden, and Bob Evan's Restaurants await on Ridge Road.

Plans are in place to extend his trail south to connect to the Erie Canalway Trail but no definitive timeline has been set.

Bike Shop: The Bike Zone, 885 Long Pond Road, Rochester (585) 225-9760

Distance Between Major Roads:

Ridge Road West (Route 104) to Maiden Lane	1.5 miles
Maiden Lane to Vintage Lane	0.5 mile
Vintage Lane to English Road	0.7 mile
English Road to Latta Road	1.1 miles
Latta Road to Janes Road	1.1 miles

Trail Directions
- From the Greece Odyssey School parking lot, turn right (N) on the sidewalk along Hoover Drive.
- Cross Hoover Drive at the traffic light on the corner of Ridge Road West (Route 104).

- Double back on the opposite side of Hoover Drive and climb the ramp of the large, brown, pedestrian bridge to cross Route 104.
- Bear right off the bridge on the paved bike path as it heads north, parallel to Interstate 390.
- Pass Greece Olympia High School sports fields on your right.
  (At the school property, a spur to the left goes up a ramp to cross Interstate 390 and ends at Fetzner Road.)
- Continue past Greece Olympia High School.
- Turn left at Maiden Lane, under the Interstate 390 bridge.
- Cross Maiden Lane at the crosswalk and continue north.
- Pass through woods and beside a creek.
- Cross Vintage Lane at 2.1 miles and bear right on the bike path.
- You'll pass dirt hiking trails, a disc golf course, and WorldTrail® exercise stations as the trail winds through Marella Park.
- Cross English Road and bear right.
- Cross Latta Road. You've ridden 3.9 miles.
- Cross a bridge over a creek.
- Cross Janes Road at 5.0 miles. (Turn right here if you plan to continue on the Ontario State Parkway.)
- At the off-ramp from Ontario State Parkway to Interstate 390, turn-around and reverse your trek. (There is no parking at this northern terminus. Heading south you'll notice things you never saw on your northward journey, and you'll get more exercise with the slight uphill rise.)

Date Enjoyed: _____

Notes:

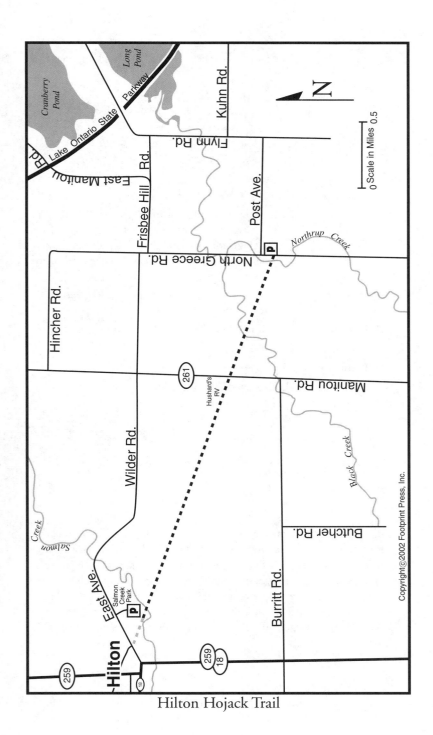

Hilton Hojack Trail

2.

Hilton Hojack Trail

Location:	Hilton to Greece, Monroe County
Parking:	From Route 259 which runs north/south through Hilton, turn east onto East Avenue. Watch for a dark sign for Salmon Creek Park on the right. The parking area is at the end of the road, near Salmon Creek.
Alternative Parking:	North Greece Road (near Geiger Towing Service, 338 North Greece Road)
Riding Time:	50 minutes round trip
Length:	5.6 miles round trip
Difficulty:	Easy
Surface:	Hard-packed dirt and cinder
Trail Markings:	None
Uses:	
Facilities:	Picnic pavilion and grills in Salmon Creek Park
Dogs:	OK on leash
Admission:	Free

Hilton and Hamlin grew as agricultural communities. They prospered with the building of the Lake Ontario Shore Railroad, better known as the Hojack Railroad, in 1876. Agricultural products shifted from grain to fruits now that a quick, easy method was at hand to get their products to market. As with many of our area railroads, the Hojack Railroad business was shifted to trucks on interstate highways and ceased operation in the late 1970s. At the time of its demise, this rail line was part of the Penn Central System.

The Hilton Hojack bridge over Salmon Creek
as seen from Salmon Creek Park.

Several segments of the old Hojack line are available for biking. This one runs between Hilton and Greece. Other segments are in the Hamlin area (see page 41), the Webster area (see page 80), and the Hannibal area (see page 107).

This is an easy-riding trail with a hard-packed dirt and cinder surface. Parking is minimal at North Greece Road so it's best to go out and back from Salmon Creek Park. This converted railroad bed is on private property with a variety of owners. Please treat the land with respect so the owners don't close the trail. If you see any posted signs, please obey them.

Distance Between Major Roads:

Salmon Creek Park to Route 261	1.9 miles
Route 261 to North Greece Road	0.9 mile

Trail Directions
• From the Salmon Creek Park parking area, head south, toward the creek.
• Take the short dirt trail uphill to the Hojack Trail.

- Turn left and cross the metal grate bridge over Salmon Creek.
- Cross a creek on a cement culvert.
- At 1.9 miles, ride through the parking lot of Hushard's RV.
- Cross Manitou Road and bear right to regain the trail.
- Cross Northrup Creek on an old bridge (you may need to walk your bike).
- Reach North Greece Road at 2.8 miles. (The trail continues east from here for only a short distance.)
- Turn around and ride back to Salmon Creek Park.

Date Enjoyed: _____
Notes:

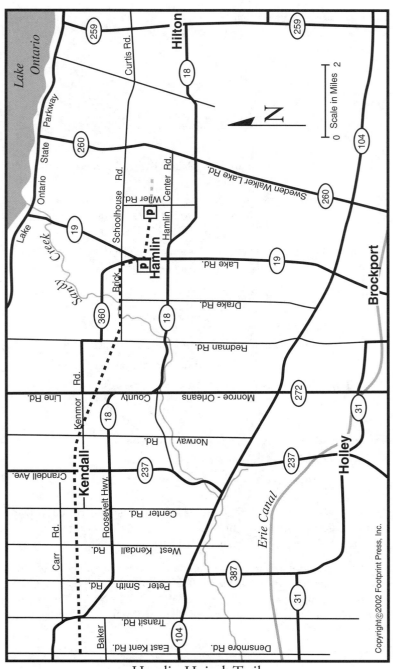

Hamlin Hojack Trail

3.
Hamlin Hojack Trail

Location:	Hamlin, Kendall and Kent, Monroe and Orleans Counties
Parking:	Along Wiler Road at the trail crossing, midway between Hamlin Center Road and Brick Schoolhouse Road in Hamlin
Alternative Parking:	Sunoco/KK Mart on Lake Road (Route 19) in Hamlin
	Any other trail/road crossing
Riding Time:	2 hours one way
Length:	14.0 miles one way
Difficulty:	Easy
Surface:	Hard-packed dirt and cinder trail
	3.2-mile paved road section (good shoulders)
Trail Markings:	None
Uses:	
Facilities:	A picnic pavilion in Morton
Dogs:	OK on leash
Admission:	Free

See pages 80, 38 and 107 for information on the Hojack Railroad and other trail segments along this abandoned railway. As with the other segments, this is an easy-riding, hard-packed trail.

There are no parking lots for this trail. Simply park along the road at any crossing (except on Lake Road in Hamlin). If you prefer to avoid the road segment, begin on Brick Schoolhouse Road near the Sandy Creek crossing and head west. You'll have 9.1 miles of trail, one-way.

This converted railroad bed is on private property with a variety of owners. Please treat the land with respect so the owners don't close the trail. If you see any posted signs, please obey them.

The easy-to-pedal Hamlin Hojack Trail.

Distance Between Major Roads:

Wiler Road to Lake Road	1.6 miles
Lake Road (Route 19) to Sandy Creek (road segment)	3.2 miles
Sandy Creek to Monroe Orleans County Line Road	2.1 miles
Monroe Orleans County Line Road to Kenmor Road	1.0 mile
Kenmor Road to Route 237 (Kendall)	1.3 miles
Route 237 (Kendall) to West Kendall Road	2.0 miles
West Kendall Road to Route 18	2.0 miles
Route 18 to East Kent Road	0.7 mile

Trail Directions

- From Wiler Road, head west on the trail. (You can ride east for 0.6 mile before the trail becomes overgrown.)
- In 1.6 miles reach Lake Road (Route 19) with a Sunoco/KK Mart across the street.
- Turn right and follow the sidewalk along Lake Road, heading north.
- Turn left when the road "Ys" to follow Route 360.
- At 3.8 miles, turn left onto Brick Schoolhouse Road.
- In another mile, cross Sandy Creek. Immediately watch for the trail to begin on the right at the red and white sign "Private Property, Trespassing at Your Own Risk."
- Cross Redman Road.
- Cross Monroe - Orleans County Line Road at 6.9 miles. Notice the Morton Fire Company picnic pavilion to your left.
- The trail wanders right to the edge of a field, then left to another field edge.
- At Kenmor Road turn left to follow the road. (The trail continues from here but it crosses two creeks and low wet areas and is unmaintained so it's easier to use the roads for a short distance.)
- At the first intersection turn right onto Norway Road.
- Shortly up the road turn left to pick up the trail again.
- At 9.2 miles cross Crandell Avenue (Route 237).
- Cross Center Road at 10.2 miles.
- Cross West Kendall Road, passing an orange "Snowmobile Trail" sign.
- At 12.3 miles cross Peter Smith Road.
- Cross Route 18 (Roosevelt Highway).
- Reach the end at East Kent Road. A red gate blocks the trail heading west from here.

Date Enjoyed: _____

Notes:

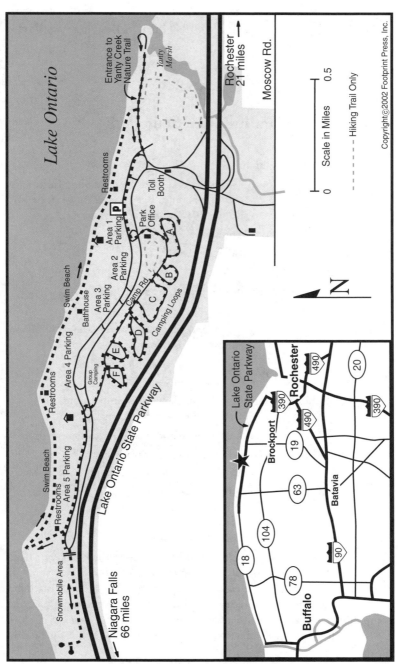

Hamlin Beach State Park

4.

Hamlin Beach State Park

Location:	Hamlin, Monroe County
Parking:	From Rochester, take Lake Ontario State Parkway west to the Hamlin Beach State Park exit (west of Route 19). Park in parking area #1.
Alternative Parking:	Lots 2 through 5
Riding Time:	1 hour loop
Length:	7.9-mile loop
Difficulty:	Easy, mostly level, some small hills
Surface:	Paved
Trail Markings:	Large brown and yellow signs mark the parking and camping areas. No markings on trails.
Uses:	
Facilities:	Restrooms, picnic pavilions, campground, play grounds, swimming beach, snack bar
Dogs:	OK if kept on a 6-foot or shorter leash at all times
Admission:	$6/vehicle May through September $5/vehicle Sept. to Thanksgiving, Fri., Sat. & Sun.
Contact:	Hamlin Beach State Park 1 Camp Road, Hamlin, NY 14464 (585) 964-2462

Hamlin Beach State Park offers a front row seat to the majesty of Lake Ontario. A paved path parallels the waterfront. Wind your way through the campground loops, then out on a barricaded road that's used by snowmobilers in winter. Return along the lake shore, passing a series of monitored swim beaches. In a few places the paved trail comes very close to water's edge so you may feel the spray if the waves are up or ride

In-line skaters enjoy the paved path along Lake Ontario in Hamlin Beach State Park.

through small patches of seaweed, evidence of previous storms. Since you're riding park roads on some segments, please be sure to wear an approved bike helmet and ride to the right, with traffic.

At the far eastern end is Yanty Creek Nature Trail. This 1.2-mile loop through a marsh is for hikers only. Please don't ride the narrow, winding, dirt trails.

This park began as part of the Monroe County Parks system in 1928 and became a state park in 1938. Its draw was the clear water and sandy beaches of Lake Ontario. Much of the building in the park was done by the Civilian Conservation Corp. During World War II, the park was used as a Prisoner of War Camp. Today, campers flock here to enjoy the wooded campsites and frolic in the lake. This is a carry-in, carry-out park so please take all trash and litter with you.

Trail Directions
- From parking area #1, follow the paved trail at the northeast corner labeled "Red Trail" by a small wooden sign.
- Ride past the red block building, heading toward Lake Ontario.
- At the shore, turn right on the paved path.
- Bear left at the next junction (the entrance to Yanty Creek hiking trails is near this junction).
- The paved path ends at a dam protecting Yanty Creek Marsh. Turn around and reverse direction.
- Bear left as the trail "Ys."
- At 0.7 mile you'll reach the main park road. Turn right.

- Pass parking area #1.
- Turn left onto Camp Road, toward the park office at the large brown sign.
- Pass the camping registration building (with restrooms).
- For the next segment you'll make a continual series of left turns, looping through each of the 6 camping areas, beginning with a left turn into camping area A.
- At 3.9 miles, you'll emerge from camping area F and again turn left on Camp Road to pass the group camping area.
- At 4.1 miles, pass a silver gate and cross the main park road to turn left on Park Road. (Since Park Road is a loop of one way roads, you want to be on the northernmost branch of the road.)
- Past parking area #5, continue straight passing barricades.
- The road bends right, passes a road to the left, and ends in a cul de sac.
- From the cul de sac, return up the same road but this time turn right onto the side road.
- The side road also ends in a cul de sac. Round the cul de sac1 and head back out.
- Turn right onto the main road and follow the road past the barricades. You've ridden 6.1 miles.
- Bear left at the barricades and enter parking area #5.
- Turn left onto a small paved trail to pass a block building that contains restrooms.
- Bear left at the first junction then bear right to head east along the lake shore.
- At 6.9 miles, pass the first swim beach and snack bar.
- Pass another swim beach with a building housing the first aid station and changing rooms.
- Cross a small bridge at 7.7 miles.
- The trail is now close to the water and may be wet and seaweedy for the last 0.1 mile.
- Turn right on the paved path to return to parking area #1.

Date Enjoyed: _____

Notes:

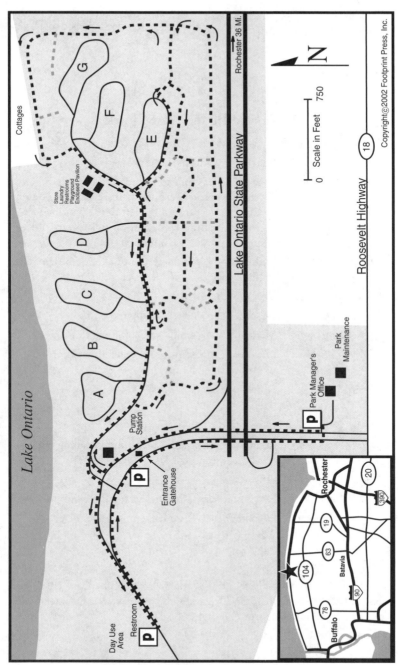

Lake Ontario

Cottages

G

F

E

D

C

B

A

Store
Laundry
Restrooms
Playground
Enclosed Pavilion

Pump
Station

Entrance
Gatehouse

P

Day Use
Area

Restroom

P

Rochester 36 Mi.

Lake Ontario State Parkway

N

Scale in Feet
0   750

Roosevelt Highway

18

Park Manager's
Office

Park
Maintenance

P

Rochester

Buffalo

Batavia

20

390

19

63

104

90

78

Lakeside Beach State Park

5.

Lakeside Beach State Park

Location:	Waterport, Orleans County
Parking:	Take the Lake Ontario State Parkway to its western end and head south, away from Lakeside Beach State Park. Park on the left in the parking area for the Seaway Trail, in front of the park office and maintenance buildings.
Alternative Parking:	In the day-use parking area in Lakeside Beach State Park (pay the $5/vehicle entrance fee)
Riding Time:	45 minute loop
Length:	4.9-mile loop on trails and park roads
Difficulty:	Moderate, gentle hills and soft grass trails
Surface:	Paved park roads and well-tended but bumpy mowed-grass trails
Trail Markings:	None
Uses:	
Facilities:	Restrooms, picnic areas, playgrounds, campground (NO swimming)
Dogs:	OK on leash
Admission:	Free for bicycles ($5/vehicle if you drive into the park)
Contact:	Lakeside Beach State Park Waterport, NY 14571 (585) 682-4888

743-acre Lakeside Beach State Park was established in 1962 and opened for camping in 1968. Originally the property was farm land with fruit orchards and lake front cottages.

You can drive into the park (paying the $5/vehicle entrance fee) or, park at the Seaway Trail parking area south of the park and bicycle in for free.

The loop described below includes riding on park roads and on grassy trails. The trails are four-feet-wide mowed swaths through a mixture of tall grasses, shrubs, and trees. The ride can be bumpy. Because the forest isn't dense, we found ourselves enjoying the graceful and varied shapes of the large trees silhouetted against the sky as we biked. Add a ride around the camping area loop roads which are labeled A, B, C, etc. to extend your biking adventure.

Trail Directions
- From the Seaway Trail parking area, head north on the park entrance road.
- Pass the entrance toll house.
- Take the first right and pass the park manager's brown house. The dogs bark, but they're friendly.
- Pass the RV pump-out station.
- At 0.6 mile, turn right onto the trail shortly after the pump-out station.
- Pass a trail to the left, then the perimeter trail bends left.
- Pass 4 more trails to the left, staying on the perimeter trail.
- The trail bends left.
- At 1.3 miles, turn left to head west and leave the perimeter trail.
- Bear left at the next junction.
- Pass a trail to the left.
- At the "T," turn left, then a quick right.
- Turn right at the next junction.
- Pass a trail to the right.
- Reach the park road at 1.7 miles. Turn right and follow the park road. (To extend your ride, bike through campground loops C and D.)
- Turn right into campground loop E and bear right at the Y.
- Ride through campsites E21 or E22 to find the trail again at the back end of campground loop E.
- At the junction, bear left.
- At the "T," turn left. The trail winds slightly downhill through woods.

- Continue straight past a blue-painted post at 2.6 miles.
- The trail bends left and passes behind cottages.
- Continue straight, passing a trail to the left.
- At the edge of a field, turn left before a stone-filled ditch.
- Turn right onto the park road. (To extend your ride, bike through campground loops F and G.)
- Pass the entrance to camping loops E, D, C, B, and A on your way back to the entrance road.
- Bear right, onto the entrance road, heading toward the day-use parking area.
- At the end, turn around in the day-use parking lot and head back up the main road.
- Bear right to follow the entrance road back to the Seaway Trail parking area.

Date Enjoyed: _____
Notes:

City Rides

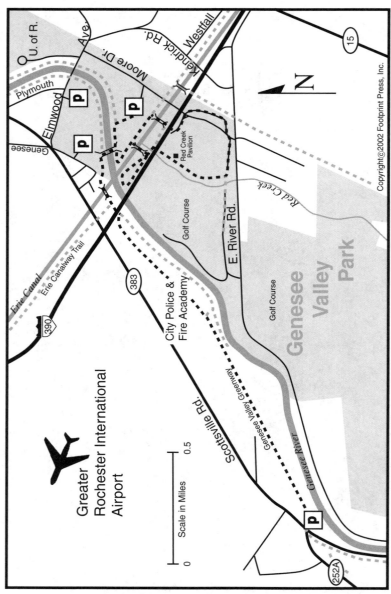

Genesee Valley Park & Genesee Valley Greenway Loop

6.
Genesee Valley Park & Genesee Valley Greenway Loop

Location:	Genesee Valley Park in Rochester to Scottsville, Monroe County
Parking:	Genesee Valley Park, off Moore Drive, near the Roundhouse Pavilion
Alternative Parking:	Genesee Valley Park off Genesee Street
	Route 383 near the intersection of Route 252A, next to Gillirmo's American Italian Restaurant
Riding Time:	1 hour round trip
Length:	7.0 miles round trip
Difficulty:	Moderate, mild hills
Surface:	Paved
Trail Markings:	Some directional signs and some Genesee Valley Greenway signs
Uses:	
Facilities:	Restrooms, picnic pavilions, snacks available at Genesee Valley Golf Club
Dogs:	OK on leash
Admission:	Free
Contact:	Monroe County Parks Department
	171 Reservoir Avenue, Rochester, NY 14620
	(585) 256-4950
	www.co.monroe.ny.us/parks/
	Friends of Genesee Valley Greenway
	6111 Visitor Center Road, Mt. Morris, NY 14510
	(585) 624-5674
	www.fogvg.org

55

One of three arched bridges over the Erie Canal and Genesee River in Genesee Valley Park.

This is a fun little loop which combines paved trails in Genesee Valley Park with a segment of the Genesee Valley Greenway. It meanders over the Erie Canal twice on beautiful arched bridges, under the overpass of Interstate 390, and along Red Creek. It passes restrooms and picnic pavilions along the way. The hills make it interesting, but the pavement makes it an easy ride. There are four arched bridges over the waterways in this section. Three span the Erie Canal and one spans the Genesee River.

This loop can be connected with the Genesee River - Downtown Loop Trail (#7) or add it to a stretch of the Erie Canalway Trail (#40).

Genesee Valley Park is one of four Rochester parks designed by famed landscape architect Frederick Law Olmsted. Olmsted's designs were revolutionary for the late 1800s. Instead of laying out precise squares and gardens, he planned clumps of woods, meandering trails, bridle paths, and spectacular views. He planted trees carefully to effect a "forested" look. This natural, quiet ambience was half of Olmsted's design philosophy. The other half was the creation of spaces for more active use, such as open areas for baseball fields, and ponds for swimming in summer and ice skating in winter. Pavilions and bridges designed in a neo-classical style separate activity areas. The other Rochester parks designed by Mr. Olmsted are Seneca Park, Highland Park, and Maplewood Park.

The Genesee Valley Greenway will eventually be a 90-mile historic and natural resource corridor which follows a transportation route that was used by the Genesee Valley Canal, from 1840 to 1878, and by the railroad, from 1880 to the mid-1960s. The former rail bed now serves as a multi-use trail open to hikers, bikers, horseback riders, cross-country skiers, and snowmobilers. Currently, 47 miles of the total 90 miles are open for use. Each year, more segments are opened.

The segment described in this route runs from Genesee Valley Park in Rochester to Route 383, near the airport. A segment from Chili to Cuylerville is described on page 204. Additional sections south of Cuylerville are described in the book *Take Your Bike - Family Rides in the Finger Lakes and Genesee Valley Region.*

From Genesee Valley Park where the Erie Canal meets the Genesee River, follow this paved trail as it snakes southwest along the Genesee River heading toward Scottsville. Along the way, you'll pass the training center for Rochester police and fire units.

The Genesee Valley Greenway Trail ends at a parking area where Route 252A meets Scottsville Road (Route 383). To connect with the next segment of the Genesee Valley Greenway currently requires a 1.7-mile ride along the shoulder of busy Route 383 then west on Route 252. See page 202.

Trail Directions
- From the parking lot, head west toward the Genesee River on the paved path.
- Turn left and bear left past the Waldo J. Nielson Bridge which spans the river (do not take this bridge).
- Turn right to cross the next bridge. This takes you over the Erie Canal. You can see arched bridges over the canal in both directions from this vantage point.
- Bear right just before the Interstate 390 overpass.

Pat and Don Cushing of Pittsford, NY are wearing florescent yellow vests to increase their visibility to others.

- The path winds through a wooded area then bends left to loop back between the north and southbound overpasses of Interstate 390.
- Bear right uphill, then turn right after Red Creek onto the paved path.
- Pass the Red Creek pavilion on your left.
- At the park road, turn left. You've completed 1 mile.
  (Side trip: At the park road you can turn right and ride to the clubhouse of the Genesee Valley Golf Club, a public course. It offers hots, hamburgers, drinks, and snacks as well as restrooms.)
- Pass the park entrance off East River Road.
- Turn left and pass two pavilions, restrooms, then Hawthorn pavilion.
- The paved path ends. Continue straight to Park Drive.
- Turn left and follow the road back to the path leading to the right, under Interstate 390 (just before the bridge over Red Creek).
- Ride under Interstate 390 and keep right as the path leads over an arched bridge over the Erie Canal.
- After the bridge turn left.
- Bear right on the paved path, passing an arched bridge.
- Then bear left to head uphill and cross the Waldo J. Nielson Bridge which arches over the Genesee River.
- After the bridge, turn left (NW). (To the right is Trail #7, the Genesee River - Downtown Loop Trail. See page 61.)
- At the "T," turn left to head over another bridge. This one spans the Erie Canal. (The former Pennsylvania Railroad bridge is to your right.)
- At 2.9 miles, continue straight (NW) at the next junction. (To the right is the Erie Canalway Trail to Lockport, see trail #40, page 240.)
- Quickly pass another trail to the right. (This is the official Genesee Valley Greenway Trail which merges shortly with the trail you're on.)
- Pass the Police & Fire Academy on your right. The Genesee River is on your left.
- At 3.6 miles, turn right just after the Academy. (Straight ahead dead ends in 0.2 mile.)
- Pass two yellow metal gates.
- At 4.8 miles, reach the Route 383 parking area, next to Gillirmo's American Italian Restaurant. Why not stop in for a treat? (To continue south on the Genesee Valley Greenway requires a 1.7-mile road ride. Cross Route 383 and turn left (W) to ride the shoulder. Cross the

Conrail Railroad tracks. Turn right (W) onto Route 252. The Genesee Valley Greenway crosses Route 252 in 0.5 mile. See the map on page 202.)
• Turn around and retrace your route back to the parking area in Genesee Valley Park.

Date Enjoyed: _____

Notes:

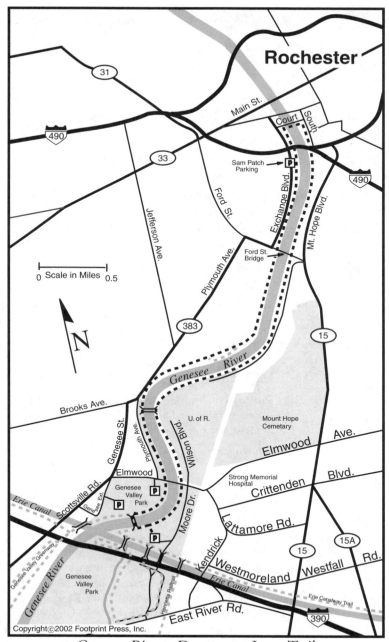

31

490

33

Rochester

Main St.

Court

South

490

Sam Patch
Parking

P

Ford St.

Exchange Blvd.

Mt. Hope Blvd.

Jefferson Ave.

Plymouth Ave.

Ford St.
Bridge

0 Scale in Miles 0.5

383

15

N

Genesee River

Brooks Ave.

U. of R.

Mount Hope
Cemetary

Elmwood Ave.

Genesee St.

Plymouth Ave.

Wilson Blvd.

Strong Memorial
Hospital

Crittenden Blvd.

Scottsville Rd.

Genesee Ext.

Elmwood

Genesee
Valley
Park

P

P

Moore Dr.

Lattamore Rd.

15A

Erie Canal

Genesee Valley Greenway

P

Kendrick

15

Genesee River

Genesee
Valley
Park

Henrietta Railroad

Westmoreland

Erie Canal

Westfall Rd.

Erie Canalway Trail

East River Rd.

390

Copyright©2002 Footprint Press, Inc.

Genesee River - Downtown Loop Trail

7.

Genesee River - Downtown Loop Trail

Location:	Genesee Valley Park through downtown, Rochester, Monroe County
Parking:	Genesee Valley Park, off Moore Drive, near the Roundhouse Pavilion
Alternative Parking:	Genesee Waterways Center, 145 Elmwood Avenue
	Genesee Valley Park, off Genesee Street
Riding Time:	1 hour
Length:	7-mile loop
Difficulty:	Easy, mostly level
Surface:	Paved
Trail Markings:	A few sporadic signs
Uses:	
Facilities:	Picnic pavilions in Genesee Valley Park, benches along trail, food at the Dinosaur Bar-B-Que Restaurant in downtown
Dogs:	OK on leash
Admission:	Free
Contact:	City of Rochester, Bureau of Parks and Recreation 400 Dewey Avenue, Rochester, NY 14613

This wonderful loop trail encompasses the Genesee Valley Park, Genesee River Trails, and sections through the University of Rochester. It takes you along the eastern side of the river heading into downtown and along the western side heading back to Genesee Valley Park. The loop described here is actually a series of trails. Portions of the riverbank trails are maintained by Monroe County, others by the University of Rochester. The Genesee River Trail is maintained by the City of

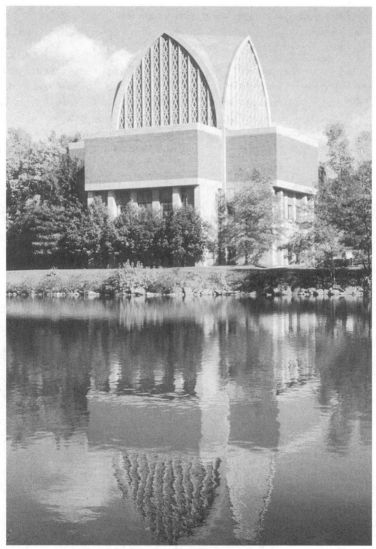

The University of Rochester chapel reflected in the Genesee River.

Rochester, Bureau of Parks and Recreation. The small section of Erie Canalway Trail is maintained by the New York State Canal Corporation. Together they've developed a perfect loop for bike riding.

As we rode, we watched the U of R sculling team practice, while workers hauled trees from the river and piled them on barges. Parts of this path on the west side of the river follow old railroad beds. In downtown you'll pass the original Lehigh Valley train station, now used by Dinosaur Bar-B-Que Restaurant. In the 1830s, before the railroads, this land held the Genesee Valley Canal, which joined Rochester with the southern tier of New York.

You'll pass through the River Campus of the University of Rochester. Construction of this campus began in 1927 after the University obtained it in a trade with Oak Hill Country Club for a portion of land east of the city. In the thirteenth century, the River Campus lands housed an Algonquin Indian village of bark cabins and farm fields.

The pedestrian bridge that spans the Genesee River has been a crossroads for decades. Rock ledges were exposed on the river bottom in this area during low water, making it a natural site for fording. Many Native American trails converged here. In the 1800s a settlement called Castletown began on the west bank. Named for the local tavern proprietor, Isaac Castle. Castletown suffered economic ruin when the Erie Canal was routed through the northern town of Rochesterville.

This ride can be shortened by cutting across the Ford Street bridge. This bridge was repaired to its early 20th century splendor in 2002 and is a beautiful sight to behold. To lengthen your ride, combine it with the Genesee Valley Park Loop (#6) or add it to a stretch of the Erie Canalway Trail (#40). For a true adventure, combine your bike ride with a ride on the boat *Sam Patch*, or rent a canoe or kayak and paddle along the Genesee River.

Genesee River - Downtown Loop Trail

Distance Between Major Roads:

Genesee Valley Park to Ford Street	2.6 miles
Ford Street (east bank) to Court Street	0.7 mile
Court Street to Ford Street (west bank)	1.4 miles
Ford Street (west bank) to Elmwood Avenue	1.7 miles
Elmwood Avenue to parking lot	0.6 mile

Tours: Sam Patch Tour Boat, PO Box 18417, Rochester, NY 14618, (585) 262-5661

Canoe/Kayak Rentals: Genesee Waterways Center, 141 Elmwood Avenue, (585) 328-3960
www.geneseewaterways.org

Looking north toward downtown Rochester
from along the Genesee River.

Trail Directions
- From the parking lot, head west toward the Genesee River.
- Bear right (N) toward the towers of the University of Rochester and Elmwood Avenue.
- As you approach Elmwood Avenue, bear left to go under the bridge.
- The path winds back to street level.
- Pass a river overlook platform.
- At the University of Rochester information kiosk, bear left, downhill.
- Pass the back of the University of Rochester chapel.
- Ride under the pedestrian bridge, then uphill along Wilson Boulevard.
- Ride under an abandoned railroad bridge.
- Notice the grand view of downtown Rochester down the river to your left.
- Pass a residential area, then the Episcopal Church Home.
- Ride under Ford Street. You are now in Genesee Gateway Park and have ridden 2.6 miles.
- Pass the South Wedge Dock and Canalside Rentals.
- Ride under Interstate 490, then turn left onto the sidewalk of South Avenue.
- Turn left onto the sidewalk of Court Street. Pass the Lehigh Valley Railroad station built in 1905, now Dinosaur Bar-B-Que Restaurant. Rundel Library is to your right. You've now ridden 3.4 miles - halfway there!
- Cross over the Genesee River, then turn left on the paved trail immediately after the river.
- Bear left past the dam and flood control structures. This dam sits on top of what used to be Upper Falls of the Genesee River.
- Ride under Interstate 490.
- Pass the South River Docking Facility. This is home to the tour boat *Sam Patch*. The historic Cornhill section of Rochester is on your right across the street.
- You are now riding parallel to the Genesee River, heading south on the west side of the river.
- Ride under Ford Street.
- Pass the Church of Love Faith Center, then old factories on your right. You're riding on the old Rochester and Southern Railroad bed.

- Pass a paved side loop to the left.
- Stay on the paved path as it heads downhill to the woods.
- The cement wall reappears parallel to the path on your left.
- Emerge from the woods parallel to Plymouth Avenue.
- Pass the University of Rochester pedestrian bridge.
- Bear left onto the asphalt path at the Genesee Valley Park sign.
- Bear left at the "Y" to go under Elmwood Avenue.
- Pass the ice rink and outdoor pool (Genesee Arena), then Genesee Waterways Center. Parking is available here.
- Proceed uphill on the paved path.
- At the first intersection, turn left. (To extend your ride, travel straight and take the next left to make a short loop.)
- Turn left and cross the Genesee River on the Waldo J. Nielson Bridge. Mr. Nielson was a leading advocate of converting abandoned railroad beds and towpaths into trails and is responsible for your being able to enjoy this ride today.
- Turn left immediately over the bridge.
- The first right toward the pavilions brings you back to the parking lot.

Date Enjoyed: _____

Notes:

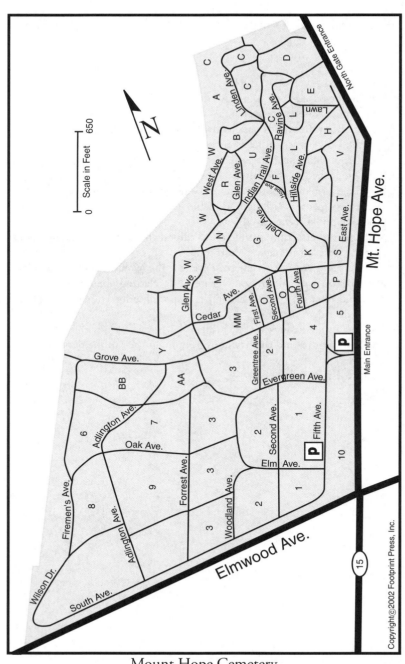

Mount Hope Cemetery

8.

Mount Hope Cemetery

Location:	Elmwood Avenue and Mount Hope Avenue, Rochester, Monroe County
Parking:	In front of the cemetery office just inside the Mt. Hope Avenue entrance
Alternative Parking:	Along Fifth Avenue within the cemetery
Riding Time:	Your choice
Length:	There are 14.5 miles of roads within the cemetery
Difficulty:	Moderate, northern part is hilly
Surface:	Paved
Trail Markings:	Some roads have old road signs. Some corners have cement posts with road names or plot numbers.
Uses:	
Facilities:	None
Dogs:	OK on leash
Admission:	Free
Contact:	Mount Hope Cemetery 1133 Mt. Hope Avenue, Rochester, NY 14620 (585) 473-2755

If you've never been to Mount Hope Cemetery, you're missing both a historical treasure and a gorgeous landscape. The roads within the cemetery are mostly narrow and paved, and although they are used by cars, the cars drive slowly making it a safe area to bicycle. The southern part of the cemetery is flat, but the northern half is a rugged area sculpted by the glaciers which covered the Rochester area millions of years ago. Mount Hope Cemetery has four large kettles, one of which (Sylvan Waters) is still filled with water. Indian Trail Avenue within the cemetery lies on an esker once used by the Seneca Indians as a major transportation route between the Bristol hills and Lake Ontario.

Kettles were created when a large block of ice separated from a glacier. Water running off the glacier deposited gravel and debris all around the ice block. The block melted, leaving behind a rough circular depression.

Eskers were formed when rivers flowed under the glacier in an ice tunnel. Rocky material accumulated on the tunnel beds, and when the glacier melted, a ridge of rubble remained.

Instead of describing a specific route within the cemetery, we're leaving you free to explore at will and create your own loops. As you can see on the map, there are many possibilities. The exploration and discovery can be part of the fun of visiting Mount Hope Cemetery. Don't worry about getting lost. It's easy to see major landmarks, and many corners are labeled to provide bearings.

Mount Hope Cemetery was established in 1838 as the first Victorian cemetery in America to be planned, developed, and maintained by a municipality. Before the nineteenth century, people were buried in the woods near villages or next to churches. During the reign of Queen

70

Victoria, a shift in attitude occurred, and death came to be considered a more romantic and celebrated phase of life, defined by the "dust-to-dust" philosophy. This led to a trend toward rural, garden cemeteries called "Victorian cemeteries."

In the 1830s a cholera epidemic hit Rochester and taxed the limits of the community and its church burial grounds. An alternative had to be found. The Rochester Common Council formed a committee to select and purchase land for a cemetery. Despite much dissension, they purchased a 54-acre plot of land one and a half miles from downtown. One of the committee members, General Jacob Gould complained that the land was "all up hill and down dale, and with a gully at the entrance at that." It's the ups and downs that make Mount Hope Cemetery such a beautiful place today.

The newly-purchased land was heavily wooded, and locals called it a howling wilderness because of its resident bears and wolves. The original forest included red, black, and white oak, chestnut, American beech, red and sugar maple, basswood, tulip tree, and white ash. Some of the trees in the cemetery today are well over 300 years old. However, many were cleared to develop burial plots. In 1847 George Ellwanger and Patrick Barry presented a gift of 50 trees from their nursery operation. Their gift included European purple, fernleaf, weeping beech, Nikko fir, Caucasian spruce, Norway maple, and variegated sycamore maple trees.

The cemetery remained unnamed for many months. A laborer named William Wilson submitted his bill using the words "for labor at Mount Hope." The name stuck and was used without any formal adoption. Over the years acreage was purchased piecemeal to increase the size of Mount Hope Cemetery, until today it covers 196 acres.

As you bike among the old trees, you'll see mausoleums, statues, gravestones, and fountains. Many of the people important in Rochester's history are buried here including Susan B. Anthony, Hiram Sibley, John Jacob Bausch, Henry Lomb, Margaret Woodbury Strong, Colonel Nathaniel Rochester, and Frederick Douglass. There are plots of veterans from the Revolutionary War, Civil War, Spanish American War, and both World Wars. To fully understand what you're seeing, we recommend the following book, available at local bookstores and libraries:

> *Mount Hope - America's First Municipal Victorian Cemetery*
> Text by Richard O. Reisem
> Photography by Frank A. Gillespie
> Published by Landmark Society of Rochester, New York
> ISBN # 0-9641706-3-9

Or, take one of the free guided tours offered during summer months by the Friends of Mount Hope Cemetery. Watch the newspaper for dates and times or call (585) 461-3494.

Date Enjoyed: _____

Notes:

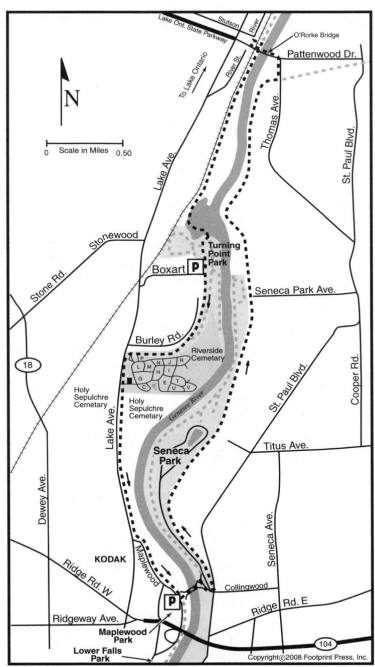

North Genesee River Trail

9.

North Genesee River Trail

Location:	The northern Genesee River gorge in Charlotte and Irondequoit, Monroe County
Parking:	The parking lot in Turning Point Park
Alternative Parking:	Near the Monroe County Pure Waters Pedestrian Bridge in Seneca Park
	Near the trail crossing on Thomas Avenue (Navy Point Yacht Sales, Thomas Storage and Fashionable Fireplaces are near this intersection)
Riding Time:	1.2 hour loop
Length:	8.7 mile loop
Difficulty:	Moderate, some hills
Surface:	Paved trails, stone dust trails, and sidewalks on the western leg, rough dirt trail on the eastern leg
Trail Markings:	Grey "Genesee Riverway" signs on the western leg
Uses:	
Facilities:	Canoe rentals in Turning Point Park
Dogs:	OK on leash
Admission:	Free
Contact:	City of Rochester Department of Parks 400 Dewey Avenue, Rochester, NY 14613 (585) 428-6770
	Monroe County Parks Department 171 Reservoir Avenue, Rochester, NY 14620 (585) 256-4950
	Riverside Cemetery 2550 Lake Avenue, Rochester, NY 14612 (585) 254-7039

The Essroc cement ship still docks at Turning Point Park.

The ride described here is a loop that combines segments of what will be longer trails. It begins in Turning Point Park and heads south parallel to the Genesee River on what the City of Rochester calls the Genesee Riverway Trail. This trail currently stops in Lower Falls Park (near Maplewood Park). The city plans to connect it, through downtown, to Genesee Valley Park. We're going to turn off this trail mid-way at the Monroe County Pure Waters Pedestrian Bridge to cross the Genesee River and cut through Seneca Park to the Rochester Running Track. Here, we'll head north on an abandoned rail bed to Thomas Avenue in Irondequoit. Follow Thomas Avenue north, then Pattenwood Drive west, crossing the O'Rorke Bridge. We'll then loop down over the railroad tracks to head south on the newly constructed northern segment of the Genesee Riverway Trail to return to Turning Point Park.

The southern Genesee Riverway Trail segment you'll ride is all paved trails and sidewalks. It's an easy ride (except for a few long hills). You can extend the easy portion of the ride by exploring the 2.5 miles of paved roads within Riverside Cemetery. Please stay on the paved roads within the cemetery. Lettered sections of the cemetery are marked by small green signs on posts. Be aware that the gates are closed at 8 PM. (Do not ride in Holy Sepulchre Cemetery - they don't welcome bicyclists or even joggers.)

Turning Point Park is a 112-acre wilderness setting in an urban environment. The term "Turning Point" has double meaning to the Charlotte residents nearby. Historically, the wide basin in the nearby Genesee River was a physical place that ships could turn around before encountering the Lower Falls. This was once a heavily used industrial area with ships visiting docks to load and unload coal, wheat, feldspar, paper boxes, and tourists. Essroc Materials, Inc., Great Lakes Cement Division still operates on this site, and uses the docks at water level to unload dry cement to the large storage tanks which sit atop the cliff.

In 1972 the Rochester-Monroe County Port Authority announced plans to build an oil storage tank farm on the site. Area residents, led by Bill Davis, fought the plan which would have bulldozed a stand of 200-year-old oak trees and cut off community access to the river. They achieved a "Turning Point" in getting the city to turn away from commercial development of the river waterfront and toward its recreational use. The city bought the land in 1976 and opened Turning Point Park in 1977. Canoe rentals are offered evenings and weekends, April through October. Call (585) 787-3370 for details. In 2006 a winding boardwalk was built over the turning basin to allow The Genesee Riverway Trail to extend northward from Turning Point Park to Lake Ontario (7.7 miles) in Charlotte. This will be part of the return portion of this loop.

History abounds along the area of the Genesee River gorge you'll traverse. The early settlements of McCrackenville, Carthage, King's Landing, Frankfort, and Castletown are all but memories. Only Charlotte remains a familiar name. With the coming of the Erie Canal, Rochesterville grew. By 1834 the combination of these seven settlements became the city of Rochester.

Once across the pedestrian bridge you'll ride the abandoned rail bed north to Irondequoit Flats. This section is rough, unimproved, dirt trail.

In 2004 the O'Rorke Bridge was built over the Genesee River, replacing the old Stutson Street bridge (which was built in 1917). The

O'Rorke Bridge is a 994-foot long lift bridge. It's named after Colonel Patrick O'Rorke, a Rochester native and Civil War hero. To read his history, see web site: http://www.ororkebridge.com/Bio.htm.

The Genesee River and the Veteran's Memorial Bridge seen from the Monroe County Pure Waters Pedestrian Bridge.

Trail Directions

- From the Turning Point Park parking area, ride south on the paved walkway toward the "Turning Point Park" sign and the brown post labeled "To Bullock's Woods."
- Pass under green pipes. (They pump dry cement from ships at the dock to the large storage tanks.)
- Continue on the paved path, passing several dirt trails heading left.
- At Lake Avenue (0.9 mile), turn left and follow the sidewalk for 1.5 miles.
- Pass Riverside Cemetery. (Turn left to explore the roads in this cemetery if you want to extend your ride.)
- Pass Holy Sepulchre Cemetery and St. Bernard's Place (a former seminary).
- Pass a paved trail to the left. (It leads to a dirt trail along the gorge used by runners.)
- Ride under the pedestrian bridge connecting Kodak Research Laboratories.
- At the corner of Maplewood Drive, turn left. Notice the old cemetery at this corner—this was the site of King's Landing, an early settlement.
- At the first break in the guardrail, turn left onto the paved path.

- Pass a bench with a great view of the Genesee River gorge. You've come 2.6 miles (assuming you didn't detour into Riverside Cemetery).
- Pass Eastman Kodak Company's King's Landing Wastewater Treatment Plant entrance.
- Pass a sign about a palisaded fort of the Indians and a grist stone from Hanford's Mill.
- Turn left to cross the pedestrian bridge over the river at the Genesee River Trail sign "Bridge to Seneca Park & Zoo."
- A long ramp will take you down to bridge level with great views of the Genesee River gorge. You've come about 3.1 miles. (If you want to stay on easy, paved trails, turn around here.)
- Ride the ramp uphill from the bridge.
- At the road, turn right and follow Parkwood Road to the entrance of Seneca Park. (Do not turn left and follow the trails within Seneca Park— they're for hikers only.)
- At St. Paul Boulevard turn left and follow the sidewalk.
- Bear left on the abandoned rail trail in 0.1 mile.
- Follow the railbed, heading northwest.
- Pass several entrances to Seneca Park on the left. (Again, trails in Seneca Park are for hiking only.)
- Pass the end of Seneca Park Avenue on the right. You're now in Irondequoit Flats.
- The trail bends right. Turn left onto Thomas Avenue. You've come 6.9 miles.
- Cross Pattenwood Drive, turn left and cross O'Rorke Bridge on the north side.
- Take the ramp down to the right, and cross over the railroad tracks to the trail between the tracks and the river.
- Head south on the trail. (Northward, it's 0.6 mile to Lake Ontario.)
- Follow the trail across the boardwalk over the turning basin and return uphill to the parking area in Turning Point Park.

Date Enjoyed: _____

Notes:

Rides Northeast of Rochester

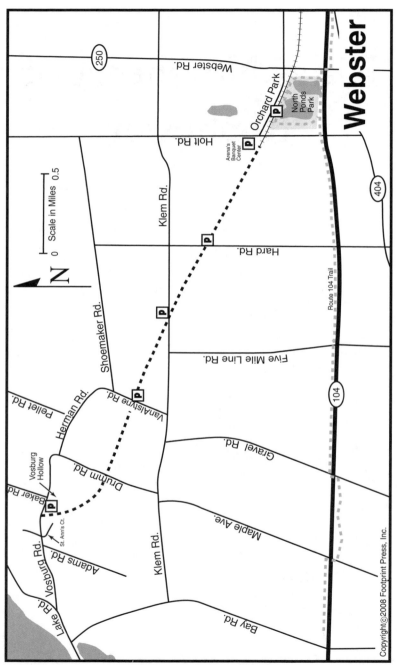

Webster - Hojack Trail

10.
Webster - Hojack Trail

Location: Between Vosburg Road and North Ponds Park, Webster, Monroe County

Parking: Arena's Banquet Center on Holt Road

Alternative Parking: At any of the road intersections. Hard, Klem, VanAlstyne and Vosburg Roads all have space for several vehicles immediately adjacent to the Hojack Trail.

Gravel parking lot on the north side of North Ponds Park, along Orchard Road.

Riding Time: 30 minutes one way

Length: 3.5 miles one way

Difficulty: Moderate, level but bumpy

Surface: Grass and cinder path over an old gravel rail bed. The trail is maintained by volunteers to a minimum width of eight feet.

Trail Markings: Wooden "Hojack Trail" signs

White markers on posts at the eastern end

Uses:

Facilities: None

Dogs: OK on leash

Admission: Free

Contact: Friends of Webster Trails
C/O Webster Parks and Recreation Department
985 Ebner Drive, Webster, NY 14580
(585) 872-7103
www.webstertrails.org

This converted railway bed terminates in the Vosburg Hollow Nature Preserve at the west end and connects to North Ponds Park at the east end. Combine your ride with a loop through North Ponds Park (page 84) and a jaunt out the Route 104 Trail (page 87) for a longer adventure.

In the 1850s the farmers of Webster had three options for shipping their produce to market. They could endure an all-day wagon ride to Rochester, an eight-mile wagon ride to the Erie Canal in Fairport, or meet a schooner at Nine Mile Point on Lake Ontario. All were arduous choices.

The prominent businessmen of Webster worked with representatives from other towns between Lewiston and Oswego to inspire the creation of the Lake Ontario Shore Railroad Company in 1868. In 1876 trains began arriving and departing from the Webster station. The line was sold to the Rome, Watertown and Ogdensburg Railroad and the abbreviations R.W. & O.R.R. became known as "Rotten Wood and Old Rusty Rails."

In 1889 a major crash occurred as a westbound train from the Thousand Islands rammed a train as it boarded passengers bound to Rochester. Many Webster homes became temporary hospitals to care for the injured. This crash brought about the use of automotive brakes on railroads.

The Webster train station became a hub of activity. In the fall, the railroad was hard pressed to supply enough cars to transport all the apples from local orchards. The Basket Factory was built along the tracks and became the largest and most productive basket factory in the world. Companies such as the Webster Canning and Preserving Company (a predecessor to Curtice-Burns), the Basket Factory, John W. Hallauer and Sons Evaporated Fruits, Martin Brothers Lumber Company, Webster Lumber Company, and LeFrois Pickling Factory, all owed their existence to the railroad.

This rail line, like all others in the area, was doomed by the increase in trucks and automobiles. Thanks to the Friends of Webster Trails it became a hiking and biking trail in 1997. To read more about the history of this rail line and the Hojack Station, check their web site at www.web-stertrails.org.

Trail Directions
- From Arena's parking lot, follow the grassy path marked by white diamond-shaped markers on posts to the right, heading away from Holt Road.
- Bear right (W) along the 8-foot-wide rail bed.
- On your right, watch for the cement pillar with a "W," telling the train conductor to blow the whistle.
- Cross Hard Road.
- At Klem Road, cross diagonally toward the right.
- Cross VanAlstyne Road.
- Pass an old cement railroad post inscribed "P87," denoting 87 miles to Pulaski. Pulaski must have been a major port on Lake Ontario in the heyday of the railroads.
- Pass a yellow metal trail barricade and cross Drumm Road.
- At Vosburg Road, turn around and retrace the path.

Date Enjoyed: _____

Notes:

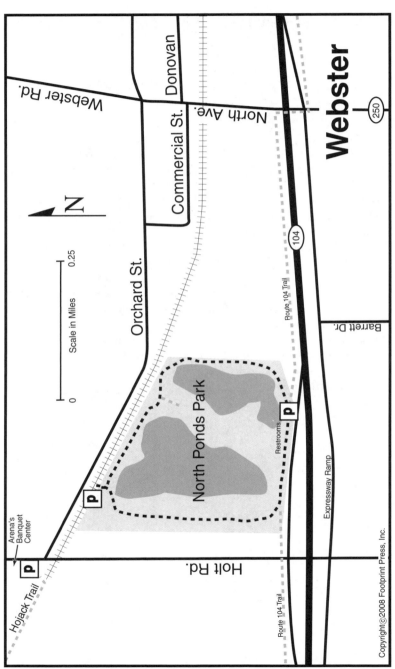

North Ponds Park Trail

11.

North Ponds Park Trail

Location:	North Ponds Park, Webster (between Route 104 and Orchard Road), Monroe County
Parking:	Free lot on Orchard Road
Alternative Parking:	Off westbound Route 104 entrance ramp off North Avenue - pay in summer (June 13 through August 31), free the rest of the year
Riding Time:	15 minutes
Length:	1.1-mile loop
Difficulty:	Easy, level
Surface:	Paved path, dirt path to Orchard Road
Trail Markings:	None
Uses:	
Facilities:	Picnic pavilion, restroom, swimming beach
Dogs:	OK on leash
Admission:	Free
Contact:	Webster Parks and Recreation Department 985 Ebner Drive, Webster, NY 14580 (585) 872-2911

North Ponds Park has a popular swimming area in summer. An easy, paved trail circumnavigates the park's two largest ponds and makes a nice ride at any time of the year (unless it's covered in snow). The area can be somewhat noisy from traffic on nearby Route 104.

To extend your ride, combine this loop with the Webster-Hojack Trail (page 80) or the Route 104 Trail (page 87).

Trail Directions
- From the parking lot on Orchard Road, follow the path into the park.
- At the "Y" junction bear right.
- Follow the path, bearing left as it winds around the ponds, past the picnic pavilion, restrooms, etc.
- Turn left after the swim area.
- Bear right at the "Y" junction. (The left path leads between the two ponds to a picnic area.)
- Turn right when you see the dirt path, to return to the parking lot.

Date Enjoyed: _____

Notes:

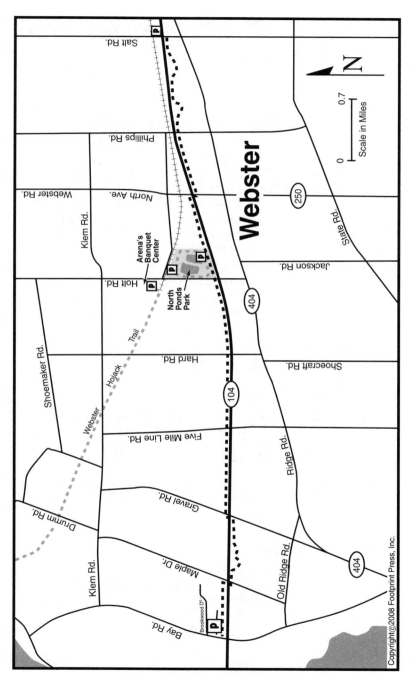

Webster - Route 104 Trail

12.
Webster - Route 104 Trail

Location: Bay Road to Salt Road, Webster, Monroe County

Parking: Near the corner of Bay Road and Route 104 (From Bay Road take a right onto Brookwood Drive. Turn right onto Bayside Drive and follow it around to the right. Park in the cul-de-sac at the end of the road.)

Alternative Parking: North Ponds Park parking lots, north of Route 104 on Orchard Road

New York State Department of Transportation parking lot on Salt Road just north of Route 104

Riding Time: 1 hour one way

Length: 6.1 miles one way

Difficulty: Easy, gentle hills

Surface: Paved

Trail Markings: Green-and-white metal signs on posts showing a bicycle and the words "Bike Route"

Uses:

Facilities: Picnic pavilion, restroom, and swimming beach in North Ponds Park, ice cream and food north on Route 250

Dogs: OK on leash

Admission: Free

Contact: Town of Webster, Town Hall
1000 Ridge Road, Webster, NY 14580
(585) 872-1000

This paved path, built in 1997, is now heavily used for recreation. It makes a great 12-mile bike journey out and back. Or, connect this trail with the North Ponds Park or Webster - Hojack Trails to create a longer adventure. Although this trail parallels Route 104, sometimes on the north, and sometimes on the south, it is a separate bike path that stays a safe distance from the busy highway. Be sure to use crosswalks when crossing roads and obey all traffic signals.

Distance Between Major Roads:

Bay Road to Maple Drive	0.9 mile
Maple Drive to Gravel Road	0.4 mile
Gravel Road to Five Mile Line Road	0.9 mile
Five Mile Line Road to Hard Road	0.7 mile
Hard Road to Holt Road	0.7 mile
Holt Road to Route 250	0.9 mile
Route 250 to Phillips Road	0.7 mile
Phillips Road to Salt Road	0.9 mile

Trail Directions
- From the cul-de-sac parking lot near the corners of Bay Road and Route 104, head around the guard rails, ride over the grass toward Route 104 and turn left (E) on the paved path.
- At Maple Drive turn right and ride under Route 104. Immediately after the bridge, cross Maple Drive and continue on the bike path south of Route 104.
- Pass several retention ponds.
- At Gravel Road, cross under Route 104 again, cross Gravel Road, and continue on the bike path north of Route 104.
- Cross Five Mile Line Road using the crosswalk and traffic light.
- Cross Hard Road. You've come 2.9 miles.
- Cross Holt Road.
- Pass through the southern edge of North Ponds Park. You can extend your ride with a loop around the ponds, stop for a swim or picnic, or visit the restrooms.

- At Route 250 (South Avenue) turn right under the Route 104 bridge. Then cross Route 250 and continue on the bike path.
  (Side Trip: North on Route 250, you'll find a Bagel Bin Café, Martino's Pizzeria, and Hank's Ice Cream Shop. South on Route 250 is Baskin Robbins Ice Cream and Dunkin Donuts.)
- Cross Phillips Road. You've come 5.2 miles.
- Pass the Holy Trinity Church cemetery and a holding pond. The path winds through the woods until it meets Salt Road.
- At Salt Road the trail ends (6.1 miles). You can turn around and head back or take a left under the bridge to find the New York State Department of Transportation parking lot just north of Route 104.

Date Enjoyed: _____
Notes:

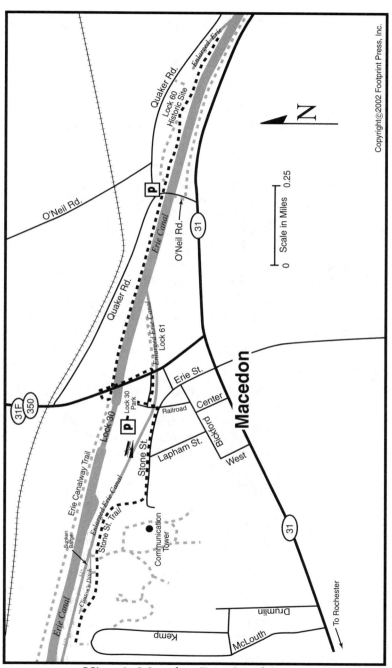

Historic Macedon Erie Canal Route

13.
Historic Macedon Erie Canal Route

Location: Macedon, Wayne County

Parking: From Route 31 in Macedon, turn north on Route 350. Before crossing the Erie Canal, turn left (W) into Lock 30 Canal Park.

Alternative Parking: Lock 60 parking area on the corner of O'Neil and Quaker Roads.

Riding Time: 45 minutes round trip

Length: 5.0 miles round trip total

(3.3 miles round trip to Lock 60)

(1.7 miles round trip on the Stone Street Trail)

Difficulty: Easy, gentle hills

Surface: Paved roads and dirt and mowed-grass trails

Trail Markings: None

Uses:

Facilities: Boat launch and picnic tables in Lock 30 Canal Park, Porta-Potty at Lock 60 parking area on Quaker & O'Neil Roads

Dogs: OK on leash

Admission: Free

Contact: Town of Macedon
30 Main Street, Macedon, NY 14502
(315) 8986-4177

Macedon Trails Committee
1009 Mayflower Drive, Macedon, NY 14502-8801
http://home.rochester.rr.com/truck1/ny/macedon.htm

Lock 60 Locktenders Association
PO Box 454, Macedon, NY 14502

Riding through Lock 60, an historic remnant from
a previous version of the Erie Canal.

This route combines trails and short road segments to visit locks and canal channels from three versions of the Erie Canal.

The Erie Canal went through a series of enlargements and re-routings from its humble beginnings as Clinton's Ditch. For simplicity, we'll focus on three major stages: Clinton's Ditch, the enlarged Erie Canal and the current Erie Canal (which for a while was called the Barge Canal). Along this route you'll visit lock 30—an operating lock on the current Erie Canal. You'll also visit locks 60 and 61 from the enlarged Erie Canal. Lock 60 was built in 1821 and was originally called lock 71 on Clinton's Ditch. It was enlarged and renamed lock 60 when the Erie Canal was enlarged in 1841. It was doubled in 1874 and lengthened in 1888. What you'll see are the well preserved stone block structure of the lock before it was abandoned in 1914 when the current Erie Canal was rerouted just south of the enlarged Erie Canal. The Lock 60 Historic Site was renovated and is maintained by a group of volunteers called the Lock 60 Locktenders Association.

Lock 61 also dates back to the early 1800s. Today it is used as a dam in the abandoned enlarged Erie Canal channel to funnel water to nearby factories. At one point on this route, you'll be able to see three canal channels: Clinton's Ditch, the enlarged canal, and the current Erie Canal. See page 98 for a short history of the Erie Canal.

Trail Directions
- From Lock 30 Canal Park, ride toward the current Erie Canal to watch boats pass through Lock 30.
- Head out the exit road, passing Railroad Avenue, to Route 31F/350.
- Cross Route 31F/350 and continue straight on a small paved side road. Look to your right to see the fast moving water in the enlarged Erie Canal channel flow through old Lock 61.
- Return to Route 31F/350, cross it, and turn right, heading north toward the current Erie Canal.
- At 0.6 mile, cross over the canal then take an immediate left on a gravel trail to access the part of Lock 30 Canal Park on the north side of the canal.
- Before the canal, turn left onto the Erie Canalway Trail and ride under the Route 31F/350 bridge.
- At O'Neil Road the Erie Canalway Trail will turn right to cross the O'Neil Road bridge. You should cross O'Neil Road and head downhill on the trail on the opposite side of the road, staying north of the canal. You're now heading into Lock 60 Historic Site. (A parking area with a Porta-Potty is just to the left at the corner of O'Neil and Quaker Roads.)
- At the 'Y,' bear right. You'll reach Lock 60 in 0.1 mile.
- Explore Lock 60 then continue east on the trail parallel to the current Erie Canal. To your left will be marshy areas and segments of the enlarged Erie Canal.
- This trail ends 0.1 mile past Lock 60 on a spit of land where the enlarged Erie Canal merges into the current Erie Canal. You've come 1.6 miles. Turn around and head back.
- Just after Lock 60 you can continue straight on the hard-packed trail you rode out on or bear right to follow a softer (and harder to pedal) mowed-grass trail which is the canal towpath from the 1850s (the enlarged Erie Canal). The two trails merge before O'Neil Road.
- Cross O'Neil Road and head west on the Erie Canalway Trail.

- Ride under the Route 31F/350 bridge and bear right to head up to Route 31F/350.
- Turn right and follow Route 31F/350 south over the canal.
- Take the first right, heading toward Lock 30 Canal Park. You've come 3.2 miles.
- Instead of continuing to the parking area, take the first left onto Railroad Avenue, cross the channel of the enlarged Erie Canal, then turn right onto Stone Street.
- Ride west on Stone Street. Just before the end, where the road bends sharply left, look to the right to see a dirt trail heading into the woods.
- Turn right and begin riding the Stone Street Trail downhill.
- The trail will bend to parallel the enlarged Erie Canal.
- Pass a sign on the right that explains the physical locations of Clinton's Ditch, the enlarged canal and the current canal.
- Pass two trails to the right and a third to the left. (0.2 mile in on the Stone Street Trail). (The trail to the left is a mowed-grass and dirt trail to the top of the hill where there's a communication tower. Side trails connect to area housing tracts. Some of these trails are on private property.)
- Stop to walk a very short trail to the right. (You'll walk on a dirt bridge between segments of Clinton's Ditch to the bank of the enlarged Erie Canal. Look carefully at the spit of land ahead of you that separates the enlarged Erie Canal from the current Erie Canal and you can see two wood and metal posts—remains of a sunken barge.)
- Continue west on the Stone Street Trail, passing two benches.
- The trail ends at a grassy area before houses. You've come 4.1 miles. Turn around and ride back to Stone Street.
- Turn left and follow Stone Street to Railroad Avenue.
- Turn left on Railroad Avenue and follow it back to Lock 30 Park.

Date Enjoyed: _____

Notes:

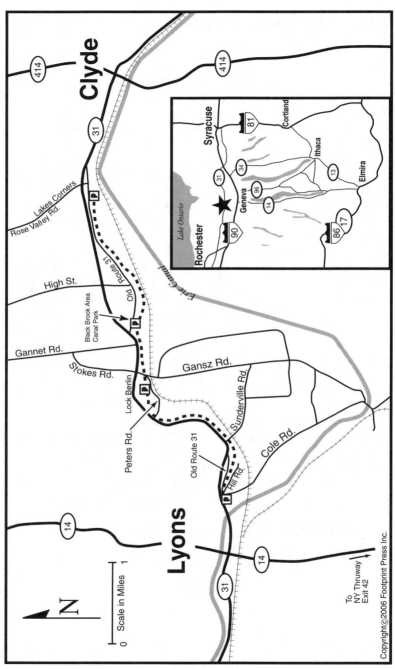

Canal Park Trailway

14.

Canal Park Trailway

Location:	Lyons to Clyde, Wayne County
Parking:	Heading east on Route 31 through Lyons, cross over the Erie Canal, then turn right onto Cole Road. Quickly turn left onto Hill Road, and park along the road near this intersection.
Alternative Parking:	Lock Berlin Park on Peters Road.
	Black Brook Area Canal Park on Old Route 31.
	Roadside at the end of the trail, near 9928 Old Route 31.
Riding Time:	1 hour one way
Length:	5.1 miles one way
Difficulty:	Moderate, some hills, soft path, beware of woodchuck holes
Surface:	Mowed-grass path
Trail Markings:	2 by 3-foot, white, blue, and faded red signs
Uses:	
Facilities:	Black Brook Area Canal Park has picnic pavilions, restrooms and a playground.
	Berlin Lock has picnic tables.
Dogs:	OK on leash
Admission:	Free
Contact:	Wayne County Planning Department 9 Pearl Street, Lyons, NY 14489 (315) 946-5919

Follow history back in time as you pedal from the existing Erie Canal to the original Clinton's Ditch of 1817 and the Enlarged Erie Canal of the 1850s. Along the way pass stone locks, long abandoned. On one trip we

A grassy trail parallels the abandoned canal bed
on the Canal Park Trailway.

saw wild turkey and a beaver repairing his den. Locals say the old canal
waters are a great fishing spot for bass and sunfish.

The Erie Canal, dubiously called "Clinton's Ditch," opened for operation in 1825. It was a 40-foot-wide water channel with locks 90 feet long
and 15 feet wide. Boats with loads up to 75 tons could navigate the waters.
By 1840 a greater capacity was needed as commerce along the canal
boomed, and the canal was enlarged to 70 feet wide. Locks increased to
110 feet long and 18 feet wide allowing cargos up to 200 tons.

By 1909, the canal was overcapacity again. This time the canal was
rerouted in places as it was enlarged. The name was changed to reflect its
growing purpose. The new-and-improved Barge Canal opened in 1918
allowing cargos of 3,000 tons to pass through its 45-foot-wide locks. The
opening of the Saint Lawrence Seaway eliminated the need to transfer
goods to barges and rendered the the canal obsolete. The name was
changed back to its historic one: the Erie Canal.

You can zip to and from this adventure on the New York State Thruway,
but why not slow down and follow Route 96 for at least one leg of the jour-

ney. You'll be rewarded with a tour through stately old towns and spectacular examples of cobblestone houses along the way. (For more information on unique local cobblestone buildings, pick up a copy of *Cobblestone Quest — Road Tours of New York's Historic Buildings*.)

Avoid riding here in spring when the trail can be wet and soft. The hills are mild, but beware of woodchuck holes. The trail used to extend another 0.7-mile west to Route 14, but that section is no longer maintained.

Trail Distance Between Major Roads:

Hill Road to Sunderville Road	0.7 mile
Sunderville Road to Peters Road	1.0 mile
Peters Road to Gansz Road	0.6 mile
Gansz Road to Black Brook Area Canal Park	0.7 mile
Black Brook Area Canal Park to Route 31	2.1 miles

Trail Directions

• From the intersection of Cole Road and Hill Road, follow the grass path between Old Route 31 and Hill Road.
• Pass an old stone bridge abutment. Clinton's Ditch is on your left.
• The trail passes through a low area that can be muddy in wet weather and may not get mowed regularly.
• Cross Sunderville Road. Clinton's Ditch continues to be on your left.
• Pass two dirt dikes across the old canal bed.
• Cross Peters Road.
• Notice the large beaver dam across the old canal bed.
• Pass an abandoned, stone, double lock. A park is at the lock (Lock Berlin) with picnic tables and grills.
• Cross Gansz Road. The canal is dammed here and becomes a trickle in a ditch from here east.
• Cross a small wooden bridge.
• A short side trail to the left leads to stonework around a feeder creek, which is actually half of an original Clinton's Ditch lock rebuilt to form a waste weir.
• A path to the left, across a crooked wooden bridge, leads to Black Brook Area Canal Park. This park has restrooms, a pavilion, picnic tables, grills, and a playground.

• The mowed path ends at a driveway. You can turn around here to head back or turn left onto the driveway (9928 Old Route 31), then right (E) onto Old Route 31, and ride 0.9 mile to the junction of Route 31 where parking is available.

Date Enjoyed: _____

Notes:

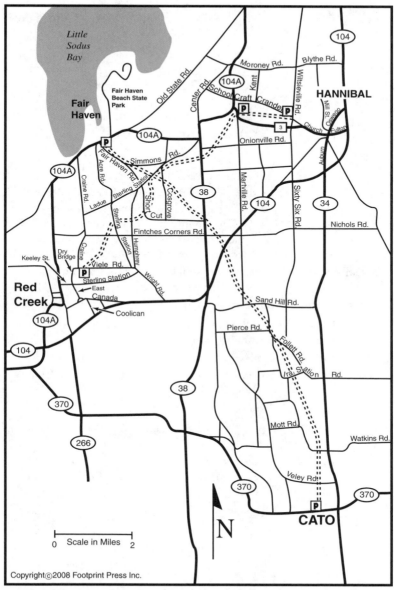

Fair Haven - Cato Trail and Hannibal - Hojack Rail Trail

15.
Fair Haven - Cato Trail
(Cayuga County Trail)

Location:	Fair Haven to Cato, Cayuga County
Parking:	Southeast side of Route 104A, Fair Haven (a dirt parking area at a brown-and-yellow sign saying "Cayuga County Trail." Located behind Screwy Louie's Sport Shop. Across the street is Hadcock Sales and Guiseppe's Sub and Pizza Shop.)
Alternative Parking:	Route 370, west of Cato (next to Cato Station, 2487 West Main Street)
Riding Time:	1.5 hours one way
Length:	13 miles one way
Difficulty:	Easy, mostly level
Surface:	Cinder, hard-packed dirt, and mowed grass
Trail Markings:	Brown signs with yellow lettering "Cayuga County Trail, Fair Haven - Cato, 14 miles"
	Road crossings have stop signs
Uses:	
Facilities:	A Porta-Potty at the Route 104A end, benches along the trail. Restaurants in Fair Haven and Cato.
Dogs:	OK on leash
Admission:	Free
Contact:	Cayuga County Planning Board 160 Genesee Street, Auburn, NY 13021-1276 (315) 253-1276
	Cayuga County Office of Tourism 131 Genesee Street, Auburn, NY 13021 (800) 499-9615 http://tourcayuga.com

Here's a pleasant country ride to get you away from urban chaos. The trail is mainly a raised bed through woods, swamps, and Christmas tree farms. It's an easy ride, shaded by a canopy of trees. In wet weather, be ready to ride through and around some puddles. The trail starts in Fair Haven, home of the 865-acre Fair Haven Beach State Park, which has cabins and camping. Consider making this trail a weekend getaway, camping at the park and biking during the day. If it's warm, bring your swimsuits for a dip in Lake Ontario at the park's beach. Enjoy a meal at the Pleasant Beach Hotel and Restaurant overlooking Little Sodus Bay, or savor the homemade pastries at the Fly By Night Cookie Company. The Cato Hotel and Tavern on Route 370 is located just one block east of the trail.

Cato is nestled among the unique glacial ridges known as drumlins. Drumlins are long, narrow, rounded hills of sediment, formed when the glaciers scoured our countryside. These ridges sit north-south across our region and resemble an old-fashioned washboard.

This rail bed was part of the Lehigh Valley Railroad, which transported coal, passengers, and farm products from Pennsylvania to Lake Ontario. The coal was processed at a big coaling facility on Little Sodus Bay and transferred to steamships. This rail line opened in 1871. The coal dock in North Fair Haven was completed in 1872, and the first coal was dug in Athens, PA, on May 16 in 1872. Unfortunately, the rail line wasn't successful, and it closed in the early 1930s, earlier than most lines. The rails north of Cato were torn up before World War II. Cayuga County acquired the right of way and built this trail in the 1980s.

Trail Distance Between Major Roads:

Fair Haven to Sterling Station Road	1.6 miles
Sterling Station Road to Route 38	2.0 miles
Route 38 to Fintches Corners Road	0.7 mile
Fintches Corners Road to Route 104	0.3 mile
Route 104 to Sand Hill Road	2.0 miles
Sand Hill Road to Follett Road	1.2 miles
Follett Road to Ira Station Road	1.1 miles
Ira Station Road to Watkins Road	2.2 miles
Watkins Road to Route 370	1.7 miles

A wetland along the Fair Haven - Cato Trail.

Fair Haven - Cato Trail

Trail Directions
- From the Fair Haven parking lot, head southeast toward the portable toilet to find the trail.
- Cross Simmons Road.
- Cross Sterling Station Road, and continue straight. The Hannibal — Hojack Rail Trail (Trail #31, see page 165) crosses here. This was part of the Hojack Rail System. The large yellow house nearby was the Sterling Station, which served both rail lines.
- Head uphill, and cross Cosgrove Road at 2.0 miles.
- Cross Route 38.
- Cross Fintches Corners Road. You've come 4.3 miles.
- The trail turns to mowed grass between Fintches Corners Road and Route 104. An old warehouse is on your right. The path parallels Queens Farms Road.
- Cross Route 104. Ride on a metal bridge over Sterling Creek. If you see signs saying "No Wheeled Vehicles," you can ignore them. They mean ATVs. Bicycles are allowed on this trail.
- Pass ponds on your left. This is a scenic spot to take a break.
- Cross Martville Road.
- Cross Sand Hill Road.
- Head downhill to cross a small creek. If you're lucky, cows will be grazing along the creek to your left.
- Cross Pierce Road. You've come 7.5 miles.
- Ride across a small bridge over a creek.
- Cross Follett Road. This is a short, rough section. A pond on the right is partly hidden by a line of trees along the trail.
- Cross Ira Station Road. To the right is Ira Corners, which was settled in 1805. By 1820 this town had two stores and a hotel.
- Continue past a beautiful pond/wetland on your right.
- Cross Watkins Road. You've come 11.1 miles.
- Cross Veley Road.
- The trail ends at Route 370. To your right is the first gristmill in Ira Corners, built in 1818 by John Hooker. The town of Cato is uphill to the left. It has a hardware store, grocery store, diner, pizza restaurant, gas station, and the Cato Hotel and Tavern.

Date Enjoyed: _____

Notes:

16.
Hannibal - Hojack Rail Trail

Location:	Red Creek to Hannibal (see map on page 101), Cayuga County
Parking:	Follow Route 104A north through Red Creek. In the village, pass Viele's Agway, and turn right at the Red Creek Fire Department onto Keeley Street. Turn left at the first intersection onto Dry Bridge / Viele Road. Park along Viele Road at the trail intersection.
Alternative Parking:	Along Route 3 at the trail crossing. Near corner of Crandall and Wiltsieville Roads.
Riding Time:	1.5 hours one way
Length:	8.5 miles one way
Difficulty:	Easy, mostly level
Surface:	Crushed cinder and mowed grass
Trail Markings:	Brown signs with yellow lettering "Cayuga County Trail"
Uses:	🚶 🚴 🏃 🐎 🛷 🎿
Facilities:	None
Dogs:	OK on leash
Admission:	Free
Contact:	Cayuga County Planning Board 160 Genesee Street, Auburn, NY 13021-1276 (315) 253-1276
	Cayuga County Office of Tourism 131 Genesee Street, Auburn, NY 13021 (800) 499-9615 http://tourcayuga.com

107

This trail was part of the Hojack Rail System, just like the Webster, Hilton, and Hamlin sections that are found on pages 80, 37, and 41 respectively. The area is rugged, and the trail winds around the hills and follows the creeks and streams, making it a more enjoyable ride than one that goes in a straight line to its destination. This trail is less used than the Fair Haven to Cato segment. There are no parking lots, so you have to park along the intersecting roads.

Work is proceeding to extend this rail trail west from Viele Road through Red Creek to Wolcott. A rough trail has been cleared but it is still too rough for biking. A gap exists where a bridge is out in Red Creek.

Trail Distance Between Major Roads:

Viele Road to Sterling Station Road	1.7 miles
Sterling Station Road to Route 38	3.6 miles
Route 38 to Martville Road	1.7 miles
Martville Road to Wiltsieville Road	1.5 miles

Trail Directions
- After parking along Viele Road, head NE. (Note: The trail going SE comes to a dead end within 0.5 mile.)
- Cross Fintches Corners Road.
- Cross a bridge.
- Dip down as you cross Sterling Station Road.
- Cross Humphrey Road.
- Cross Short Cut Road.
- The trail comes out onto Sterling Station Road for a short distance to skirt private property.
- At the split-rail fence bear right to regain the trail heading toward Hannibal. You'll cross the Fair Haven to Cato section of Cayuga County Trail (Trail #30). You are now riding parallel to Sterling Station Road.
- Cross Cosgrove Road. The trail veers east, away from Sterling Station Road.
- Cross a bridge.
- Cross Route 38.
- Cross another bridge.
- Cross Onionville Road.

108

- Cross Martville Road. Parking is available here.
- Cross another bridge.
- The trail ends at Wiltsieville Road. (Beyond this the trail continues for 0.1 mile, then it's blocked and labeled "no trespassing.")

Date Enjoyed: _____

Notes:

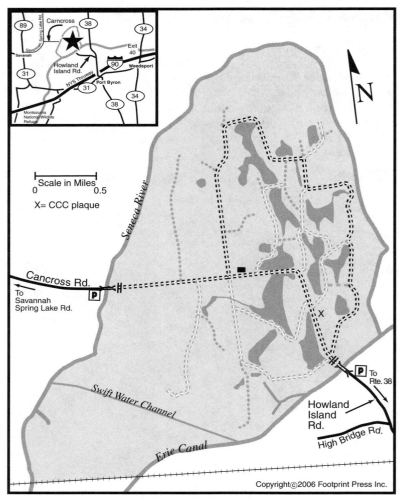

Howland Island

17.
Howland Island

Location:	Three miles northwest of Port Byron, Cayuga County
Parking:	From Port Byron (between exits 40 & 41 on the NYS Thruway) head north on Route 38. Turn west on Howland Island Road, and follow it to the closed bridge. Park along the right side of the road, before the bridge.
Alternative Parking:	At the end of Carncross Road.
Riding Time:	2 hour loop
Length:	7.8-mile loop
Difficulty:	Difficult, hilly
Surface:	Dirt, gravel and grass trails
Trail Markings:	None
Uses:	
Facilities:	None
Dogs:	OK on leash
Admission:	Free
Contact:	Howland Island Wildlife Area NYS Department Of Environmental Conservation 1285 Fisher Avenue, Cortland, NY 13045 (607) 753-3095 www.dec.state.ny.us

Waters of the Seneca River and the Erie (Barge) Canal surround the 3,100 acres of Howland Island. The land was first settled and cleared for farming in the 1800s, and farming continued until the 1920s. The land was purchased as a game refuge in 1932, and became a Civilian Conservation Corps (C.C.C.) camp between 1933 and 1941. The C.C.C.

111

The upland trails on Howland Island are tree-shaded and hilly.

built 18 earthen dikes to create about 300 acres of water impoundments.

The rolling hills and steep drumlins above these impoundments are now home to a second growth mixture of hardwoods, such as maple, ash, willow, basswood, black locust, oak, and hickory. The trails are abandoned gravel roads and old service vehicle tracks, now sufficiently packed to make pleasant biking trails. The route described here uses gravel roads for the predominately uphill section and packed grass trails for the predominately downhill section.

Through the 1930s and 1940s, Howland Island was home to an extensive pheasant farm operation that produced both eggs and pheasants. In 1951, a special waterfowl research project was begun to propagate duck species exotic to New York. Since 1962, the area has been managed for the natural production of waterfowl.

Hunting is allowed on portions of Howland Island, so be sure to wear colorful clothing if you venture out during May or from mid-October through November. If you encounter signs saying "Baited Area, hunting or entry within posted area prohibited," you can ignore them. Personnel from

112

The lowland trails on Howland Island offer easy family biking.

the D.E.C. clarified that hunting is prohibited in these areas, but walking and bicycling are allowed.

Trail Directions
- From Howland Island Road, ride across the bridge over the Erie Canal.
- Pass a grass trail to the right. (This will be part of your return loop.)
- At 0.7 mile, pass a trail to the right, then a grass trail to the left. Continue straight on the gravel road.
- Pass a yellow metal gate at 0.9 mile.
- Reach a "T" and turn left.
- Pass lily ponds and head uphill.
- Pass a D.E.C. building to the right, then pass an intersection.
- Climb another hill, and pass a trail to the left.
- Pass a trail to the right.
- Reach a water channel, earthen bridge, and yellow barricade. (Beyond here is the alternate parking area.)
- Turn around, and follow the gravel road back past two trail junctions.
- At the third trail, turn left on two gravel tracks.
- Pass a trail to the right.
- Bear right at a "Y."

- Pass a pond on the right.
- Ride between two ponds.
- Pass a trail on the right.
- At 3.7 miles, reach a "T" and turn right (S).
- At the next intersection, turn left off the gravel tracks, riding uphill on a grass trail.
- You'll enter a pleasant green tunnel and a long gradual downhill.
- Pass a pond.
- Reach a "Y" and bear left past a pond.
- Continue straight past a trail junction.
- Pass another pond.
- Pass a yellow metal gate.
- Reach the gravel road, and turn left to cross the Erie Canal bridge back to the parking area.

Date Enjoyed: _____

Notes:

Rides Southeast of Rochester

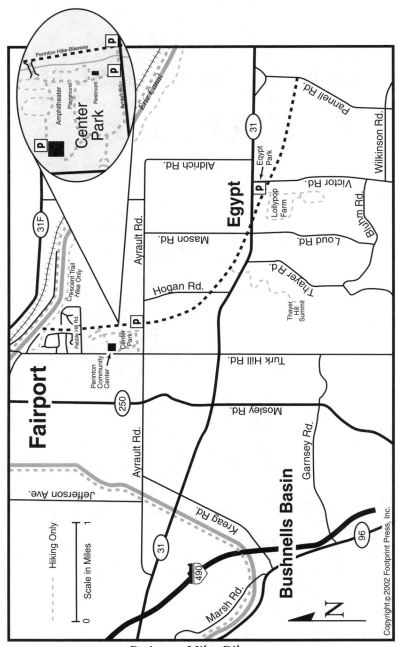

Perinton Hike-Bikeway

18.

Perinton Hike-Bikeway

Location:	Erie Canal to Pannell Road, Perinton, Monroe County
Parking:	Egypt Park on Victor Road, near the corner of Pittsford-Palmyra Road (Route 31)
Alternative Parking:	At the trail crossing on Ayrault Road or in Center Park on Ayrault Road
Riding Time:	35 minutes one way
Length:	4.4 miles one way
Difficulty:	Easy, level
Surface:	Packed stonedust
Trail Markings:	Green-and-white signs at road intersections: "No Motorized Vehicles on Hike-Bikeway" "Rochester, Syracuse, & Eastern Trolley Trail"
Uses:	
Facilities:	Restrooms in Egypt Park and Center Park
Dogs:	OK on leash
Admission:	Free
Contact:	Town of Perinton Recreation and Parks Department 1350 Turk Hill Road, Fairport, NY 14450 (585) 223-5050

The path you will ride once carried two electric trolley lines operated by the Rochester, Syracuse, and Eastern Rapid Railroad from 1906 until 1931. It was part of the Beebe Syndicate, a group of 12 high-speed, interurban, electric train lines which ran from Buffalo, through Rochester and Syracuse, then north to Oswego. The Rochester, Syracuse & Eastern Rapid Railroad portion ran from downtown Rochester to

Auburn through East Rochester, Fairport, Egypt, Palmyra, Newark, and others. A car house was located between Port Gibson and Newark. The dockmaster building in the village of Fairport is a renovated trolley stop building that was saved and moved to Fairport.

In 1908 the fare from Fairport to Rochester was $0.15 one way and $0.25 round trip. People of the time complained about the excessive fees. The RS&E cost $144,000 per mile to build (far more than an average railroad) and never made a profit in its short 25-year history. There were three reasons for its failure to prosper. First, it competed with an existing steam railroad and was never able to garner enough lucrative freight business. Second, its initial cost was too great for its earning capacity. And, finally, like all interurbans, it lost out to competition from the gasoline engine, as cars became the transportation mode of choice.

East Rochester was changed by the RS&E. Originally established as the town of Despatch in 1893, the townsfolk voted to change their name after the trolley came to town. A substation in the village still bears the Despatch name and is used today by Xerox Corporation.

Today the Perinton Hike-Bikeway traverses suburban backyards and remote woods. Before or after your ride, enjoy the restrooms, tennis courts, picnic tables, and swing sets in Egypt Park. A must for any visit is a walk around the animal pens of Lollypop Farm to see horses, ponies, donkeys, llamas, English fallow deer, geese, ducks, goats, and sheep. For a donation of $1.00 you can enter the petting area with llamas and goats. The animal shelter building houses dogs and cats looking for new homes.

English fallow deer at Lollypop Farm.

Behind the pet cemetery, a 1.3-mile loop hiking trail leads up a hill. See *Take A Hike - Family Walks in the Rochester Area* for a map and directions.

There is no parking at either end of this trail. The route described leaves from Egypt Park, heads northwest to the Erie Canal. It then reverses, goes past the start point, and heads toward the eastern end at Pannell Road. Once again it reverses and returns to the start at Egypt Park. So, a round trip (8.8 miles) is achieved from a parking spot midway between the ends of the trail.

Add to your trip by riding the new loop trails within Center Park, behind the Perinton Community Center. Center Park also has restrooms, a playground, hiking trails, and an amphitheater where concerts are held during the summer. Plans are in place to build a bridge over the Erie Canal within the next few years. This will connect the Perinton Hike-Bikeway to the 94.5-mile long Erie Canalway Trail.

Distance Between Major Roads:

Egypt Park to Hogan Road	1.3 miles
Hogan Road to Ayrault Road	0.7 mile
Ayrault Road to Erie Canal	1.1 miles
Egypt Park to Pannell Road	1.3 miles

Trail Directions

- From the parking lot at Egypt Park, head to the path at the far corner (SW).
- Follow this path over a wooden bridge.
- Turn right (W) on the wide bike path. Straight ahead is the path to Lollypop Farm.
- Cross Pittsford-Palmyra Road (Route 31).
- Cross through the front of the parking lot at the Egypt Fire Department.
- Cross Mason Road and continue on the eight-foot-wide, crushed stone bikeway.
- Cross Hogan Road.
- Cross Ayrault Road. In 1812 Egypt's first tavern and stagecoach stop was built along here. The building was moved in 1985 and is now the Oliver Loud Country Inn on the canal in Bushnells Basin.

- Pass a paved trail to the left which leads to Center Park. (Or, turn left to ride the loop trails within the park.)
- Cross Pebble Hill Road.
- The path ends at the Erie Canal and the intersection with an orange-blazed Crescent Trail. Do not bike on the orange trail.
- After enjoying the canal, turn around and retrace your path.
- Continue past the Egypt Park and Lollypop Farm side trails.
- Cross Victor Road.
- Continue on the raised bed, through a swamp area filled with cattails and the trunks of many dead trees.
- The western end of the trail arrives at the yellow posts before Pannell Road. (0.6 mile to the right down Pannell Road you'll find Chase Farms. In summer and fall (9 AM - 8 PM) they sell fresh strawberry and peach shortcakes to-die-for, as well as fresh produce and ice cream.)
- Turn around and retrace your path back to Egypt Park.

Date Enjoyed: 8 | 9 | 14

Notes:

Very enjoyable ride
Strawberry short cake @
Chase Farms — Yum!

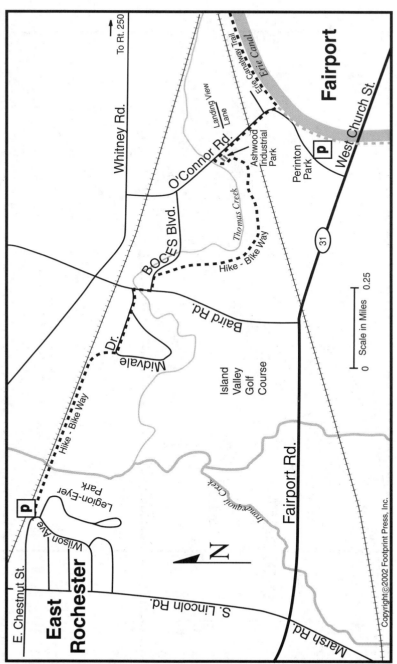

Western Hike-Bikeway to Thomas Creek Wetlands (1st segment)

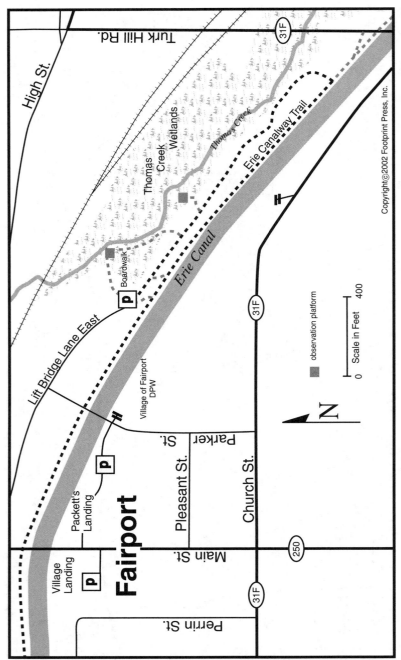

Western Hike-Bikeway to Thomas Creek Wetlands (2nd segment)

19.
Western Hike-Bikeway to Thomas Creek Wetlands

Location:	East Rochester to Fairport, Monroe County
Parking:	From Route 31F (Fairport Road) head north on South Lincoln Avenue into East Rochester. Turn right (E) on Wilson Avenue and park at the corner of E. Chestnut Street and Wilson Avenue in East Rochester.
Alternative Parking:	In Legion-Eyer Park off Wilson Avenue in East Rochester
	Perinton Park off Fairport Road
	Thomas Creek Wetlands parking area at the end of Liftbridge Lane in Fairport
Riding Time:	1 hour round trip
Length:	3.0 miles one way or 5.7 miles round trip
Difficulty:	Moderate, some small hills
Surface:	Crushed stone and paved paths connected by paved roads
Trail Markings:	None. Sign at O'Connor Road end reads "Trolley Trail." Sign at East Rochester end reads "No Motorized Vehicles Allowed on Bike-Hike Way."
Uses:	
Facilities:	Restaurants and ice cream in Fairport
Dogs:	OK on leash
Admission:	Free
Contact:	Village of Fairport
	31 South Main Street, Fairport, NY 14450
	(585) 223-0313

New York State Canal Corporation
200 Southern Blvd., P.O. Box 189
Albany, NY 12201-0189
1-800-4CANAL4
http://www.canals.state.ny.us

Bicycle an old trolley bed, a canal towpath and through a wetland all in one trip. Begin your journey in East Rochester following the route of the Rochester, Syracuse, and Eastern Rapid Railroad which operated from 1906 until 1931 (see more details under trail #18 on page 117). You'll have two short segments on roads between sections of trolley path. Then follow the Erie Canalway Trail through the heart of Fairport and finish with a loop through Thomas Creek Wetlands. Stop to walk the boardwalks and enjoy the observation decks which offer vantage points for observing the plants and animals of this wetland. See if you can spot painted turtles, muskrat and ducks swimming among the cattails. Listen for the song of wood frogs or wait for a train to pass. Just behind this 13-acre park is a very active rail line (85 trains/day) used by freight trains and the Amtrack passenger line.

Ice Cream: Lickety Splits Ice Cream is in the Box Factory building, 6 North Main Street, Fairport, (585) 377-6250

Distance Between Major Roads:

Wilson Avenue to Baird Road	0.7 mile
Baird Road to O'Connor Road	0.6 mile
O'Connor Road to Main Street, Fairport	1.0 mile
Main Street, Fairport to Thomas Creek Wetlands	0.5 mile
Trail in Thomas Creek Wetlands	0.2 mile

Trail Directions
• From the end of Wilson Avenue at the edge of Legion-Eyer Park, head southeast on the trail.
• Cross over Irondequoit Creek.
• The trail bends right and meets paved Midvale Drive at 0.5 mile.

- Turn left and follow Midvale Drive.
- Cross Baird Road and turn right to follow Baird Road for a short distance.
- Turn left onto Boces Boulevard.
- Shortly, bear right off Boces Boulevard onto the trolley trail again.
- Pass BOCES and follow the trail for 0.6 mile as it winds through the woods.
- Bear left, passing behind the Ashwood Industrial Park. Follow its property line to a break in the fence marked by a "Trolley Trail" sign.
- Turn right to follow O'Connor Road.
- At the canal, turn left and follow the Erie Canalway Trail northeast, toward the village of Fairport. You've come 1.5 miles.
- In the village ride through the tunnel under Main Street Fairport. This requires walking your bike down one flight of stairs. The bridge over the canal here is the only sloped lift bridge remaining in the world.
- Just past the bridge, pass Lift Bridge Cafe and Lickety Splits Ice Cream on your left.
- Continue on the Erie Canalway Trail, under the Parker Street bridge.
- Pass a trail to the left (to Lift Bridge Lane), a second trail to the left (to Thomas Creek Wetlands) and continue straight to the third trail to the left into Thomas Creek Wetlands. Turn left here onto the stone dust trail. You've come 2.7 miles.
- Loop back to the left and pass two boardwalks to observation platforms on the right. Please do not bicycle on the boardwalks. Park your bike and walk them to observe the wetlands.
- At the parking area, turn left to return to the Erie Canalway Trail.
- Turn right on the Erie Canalway Trail and reverse your route back to East Rochester.

Date Enjoyed: _____

Notes:

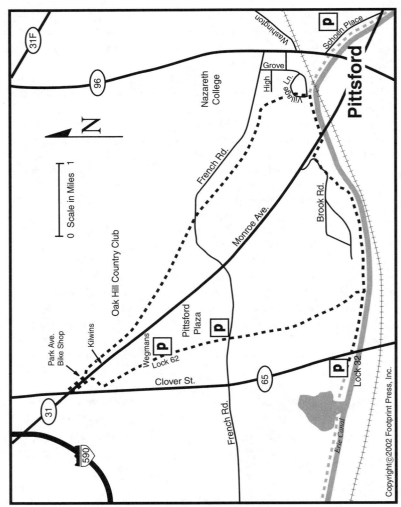

Historic Erie Canal and Railroad Loop Trail

20.
Historic Erie Canal and Railroad Loop Trail

Location:	Pittsford, Monroe County
Parking:	Lock 32 Canal Park parking area, Clover Street (Route 65)
Alternative Parking:	French Road, near Clover Street
	Lock 62 Canal Park in Wegman's parking lot at Pittsford Plaza
Riding Time:	50 minutes
Length:	6-mile loop
Difficulty:	Moderate, mostly level, some hills & steps
Surface:	Mowed grass path, paved path
Trail Markings:	Some green and white "Pittsford Trails" signs
Uses:	
Facilities:	Ice cream and bike shops, picnic tables
Dogs:	OK on leash
Admission:	Free
Contact:	Pittsford Parks Department
	35 Lincoln Avenue, Pittsford, NY 14534
	(585) 248-6280

As the name of the trail implies, you will be biking on not one, but two historic paths of transportation. The original Erie Canal, known as Clinton's Ditch, headed north to Rochester. It was opened in 1822, enlarged in the 1850s, and closed in 1920. Mules and horses pulled the canal boats on a towpath next to the canal. You'll bike on some of the old towpath. The rest is now Interstates 590 and 490. Along the way, you'll see evidence of the Odenbach Shipyard, which made barges for use on the Erie Canal and later, landing craft during World War II. You'll pass

Lock 62, built in 1870 as part of the first canal expansion and abandoned in 1920 when the new canal was routed south of Rochester.

You'll pass the Spring House Restaurant, a lovely federal-style building built in 1829 or 1830 as an Erie Canal Inn. At its peak, this area included a resort and spa with a healing sulphur and mineral spring, an amusement pavilion, and bowling alleys.

Then it's on to the Rochester and Auburn rail bed, an active railroad from 1840 through 1960. It was the first railroad east of Rochester and became part of the New York Central System. Unfortunately, Pittsford has recently allowed parking lots to be built over segments of this trail.

The third leg of the trip takes you along the present-day Erie Canal for a scenic ride back to Lock 32 Canal Park. Lock 32 was built in 1912 and still operates today.

Bike Shop:	Park Avenue Bike Shop, 2900 Monroe Avenue, (585) 381-3080
	Towpath Bike Shop, 3 Schoen Place, (585) 381-2808
Ice Cream:	Bill Wahl's Ice Cream & Yogurt, 45 Schoen Place, (585) 248-2080
	Cold Stone Creamery in Pittsford Plaza, (585) 586-9240
	Ben & Jerry's Pittsford Village, 5 S. Main Street, (585) 641-0735

Distance Between Major Roads:

Lock 32 Canal Park to French Road	1.2 miles
French Road to Monroe Ave	0.7 mile
Monroe Ave to French Road	1.4 miles
French Road to Erie Canalway Trail	1.0 mile
Erie Canalway Trail to Lock 32 Canal Park	1.7 miles

Trail Directions

• Begin by heading east on the paved canal towpath. Walk your bike down a flight of stairs. Cross underneath Route 65, where you have a great view of the bottom of a lock and gate.

128

- After 0.4 mile the path heads slightly inland from the canal. Make a sharp left turn (N) off the paved path onto a mowed-grass path at the map post showing the "Historic Erie Canal & Railroad Loop Trail."
- As you're riding on the 20-foot-wide grass path, notice the remains of the old canal bed on your left.
- The path becomes an old asphalt road. Remains of the Odenbach Shipyard are on the left.
- Cross French Road and the trail parking area. The trail narrows to 6 feet.
- The rear of Pittsford Plaza emerges on your right.
- The access trail down to Wegmans' parking lot is on the right.
- Dual Lock 62 is on your left.
- Follow the trail down steps and then over a small wooden bridge.
- Turn right after the bridge. (Trail to the left leads to homes.)
- Now you're riding in the old canal bed.
- The trail exits at the Spring House Restaurant parking lot.
- Head through the parking lot to the sidewalk along Monroe Avenue. Turn left and follow the sidewalk to the intersection of Clover Street.
- Cross Monroe Avenue. Be sure to use the crosswalk on this busy street.
- Turn right (E) onto Monroe Avenue along the sidewalk. The trail begins again behind Park Avenue Bike Shop in Clover Commons. This next segment of the trail is on the old Rochester and Auburn rail bed. There are some short, rough sections on ballast stone.
- The trail passes behind many buildings on Monroe Avenue and crosses the rear parking lots of some stores before heading off as trail again.
- Cross French Road and continue along the railroad bed.
- A cement pillar with a "W" is on the left. It alerted the train conductor to blow his whistle.
- As you approach a red brick, commercial storage building, take the trail to the right (SE).
- Turn left at the "T" junction at a pine forest. Ride toward a red-brick building.
- Turn right on the paved road and follow it around to the canal towpath, keeping the round, red-brick building on your left.
- Pass picnic tables and turn right (W) onto the canal trail. (Left goes into the village of Pittsford where you can find restaurants, ice cream shops and a bike shop.)

- Ride under the Monroe Avenue bridge.
- Follow the canal-trail signs and turn right at the NYS Canal Maintenance property.
- Take a left onto Brook Road.
- Turn left at the yellow metal gate to complete the detour around the NYS Canal Maintenance property and return uphill to the towpath along the canal.
- Follow the canal towpath to Lock 32 Canal Park.

Date Enjoyed: _____

Notes:

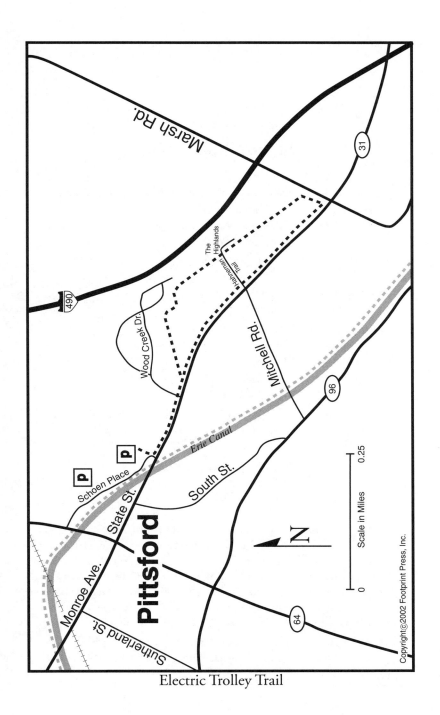

Electric Trolley Trail

21.
Electric Trolley Trail

Location:	Just east of the village of Pittsford, near Route 31, Monroe County
Parking:	Park in Northfield Commons, 50 State Street (at the east end of Schoen Place)
Alternative Parking:	Schoen Place parking lot, near the Coal Tower Restaurant
Riding Time:	20 minutes
Length:	1.8-mile loop
Difficulty:	Easy, rolling hills
Surface:	Half paved, half dirt path
Trail Markings:	None
Uses:	🚶 🚲 🏃 ⛷
Facilities:	Ice cream and restaurants near Schoen Place
Dogs:	OK on leash
Admission:	Free
Contact:	Pittsford Parks Department 35 Lincoln Avenue, Pittsford, NY 14534 (585) 248-6280

This short loop begins in the village of Pittsford and follows rolling hills parallel to Route 31. At Marsh Road it turns into a dirt path and follows the previous route of the Rochester and Eastern Rapid Railway, which operated an electric trolley from 1903 until 1930. This was a popular route from Rochester to Geneva with 36 stops between the cities. For historical photos and the history of this trolley line see web site http://www.redsuspenders.com/~dgardner/rande.html.

Trees are labeled along the way with names like shag bark hickory, black oak, Norway maple, and black cherry. This trail can be connected with the Erie Canalway Trail (the towpath) to make a jaunt as long as you wish.

There are lots of shops and restaurants for you to enjoy in Northfield Commons and along Schoen Place.

Bike Shop:	Towpath Bike Shop, 7 Schoen Place, (585) 381-2808
Ice Cream:	Brad & Dad's Homemade Ice Cream, Schoen Place
	Bill Wahl's Ice Cream & Yogurt, 45 Schoen Place, (585) 248-2080

Trail Directions
- From the Northfield Commons parking lot, ride east on the sidewalk along State Street, heading away from the Erie Canal. State Street turns into Pittsford-Palmyra Road (Route 31) as it leaves the village limits.
- Pass Wood Creek Drive. The paved bike path heads inland a bit so you're parallel to Route 31 behind a grove of trees. A farm field is on your left.
- Pass Hahneman Trail, the road to the Highlands of Pittsford.
- The path bends left (N) as it nears Marsh Road.
- At a sign for the Rochester and Eastern Rapid Railway, the pavement ends. Turn left onto the old trolley bed. You are in a pleasant tunnel of trees.
- Twice you pass entrance roads to the Highlands of Pittsford as the trail becomes more hilly.
- The path winds left and crosses a field, parallel to power lines.
- Turn right when it intersects the paved path again, and follow the sidewalk back to Northfield Commons.

Date Enjoyed: _____

Notes:

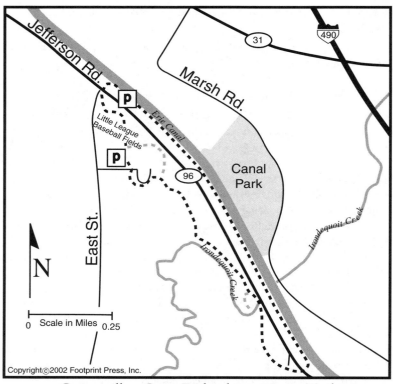

Cartersville - Great Embankment Loop Trail

134

22.
Cartersville - Great Embankment Loop Trail

Location:	Along the Erie Canal and East Street, Pittsford, Monroe County
Parking:	Little League parking lot off East Street, near the corner of Jefferson Road (Route 96)
Alternative Parking:	Route 96 near East Street next to the canal
Riding Time:	30 minutes
Length:	2.4-mile loop
Difficulty:	Moderate, three short but steep hills
Surface:	Mowed-grass and dirt trail
Trail Markings:	White and blue blazes, round metal "Pittsford Trails" markers
Uses:	🚶 🚲 🏃
Facilities:	Picnic tables along Irondequoit Creek and the canal
Dogs:	OK on leash
Admission:	Free
Contact:	Pittsford Parks Department 35 Lincoln Avenue, Pittsford, NY 14534 (585) 248-6280

The area you will ride is steeped in history. Once the site of Cartersville, a busy nineteenth century canal port, it had a distillery, warehouses, and a facility for changing the mules and horses that towed the canal boats.

You'll ride on top of the Great Embankment, one of the greatest achievements of the pioneer canal builders. Their challenge was to have the canal span the 70-foot-deep, one-mile-wide Irondequoit Creek Valley. They used earth from the area to form mounds to join the natural glacial meltwater hills of the Cartersville esker. The Great Embankment

135

was originally built in 1821-22 and was enlarged several times. The Great Embankment is the longest embankment on the Erie Canal. Only the embankment at Holley is higher.

Two guard gates, one just west of the trail and one just east of the I-90 bridge at Bushnells Basin, isolate this section of canal in case of leaks or breaks in the embankment, as happened in 1974 when contractors tunneling under the embankment, inadvertently pierced the waterway. Forty homes were damaged or destroyed as the waters rushed downhill through a 100-foot hole in the bottom of the canal before the gates could be closed. As you cross the embankment, watch for manhole covers next to the canal. These provide access to ladders in a shaft leading to the base of the concrete embankment trough, so that engineers can periodically check the embankment for leaks.

The section of Irondequoit Creek that you'll pass was once home to Simon Stone's gristmill and sawmill. Mr. Stone, a Revolutionary War veteran and founder of Pittsford, built his mills in the early 1790s. Milling in this area continued until 1913, when the canal enlargement displaced the mills.

The trail follows close to the edge of the canal; watch small children carefully.

Trail Directions
• From the parking lot, head south over the grass toward the white blaze.
• Head up the grass hill and follow the blazes around the outside perimeter of a former dump, now grass-covered. Or, follow the paved town maintenance road and turn right onto the gravel maintenance road.
• Bear right as the trail heads downhill, just before the end of the dirt road.
• A blue-blazed trail enters from the left. It is a shortcut back to the baseball fields.
• Continue straight on the white-blazed path through the woods.
• Irondequoit Creek appears on the right. Jefferson Road (Route 96) is above you on the left.
• A path veers off to the right. For a short side venture, leave your bike and follow this path down some steps to Irondequoit Creek and a picnic

A break at the picnic table where Irondequoit Creek
flows under Route 96 and the Erie Canal.

table. The culvert you'll be looking at takes the creek under Route 96 and the canal. It was built in 1916.

- Back on the white-blazed trail, wind through the woods. Toward the top of a steep hill is a yellow metal barricade off Route 96, but bear right and continue uphill.

- When you reach Route 96, cross it very carefully and turn left. The trail from here follows the south side of the canal very closely. If you have small children, you may want to walk the bikes. A right turn would connect into the Crescent Trail, but biking is not permitted.

- The towpath (Erie Canalway Trail) is on the opposite side of the canal. The canal along this section has high cement walls and banked sides. This is the highest point of the Great Embankment. Where the canal wall bows out was the site where the canal walls burst and caused a massive flood in 1912.

- Follow the mowed-grass path along the edge of the canal.

- Pass through a wooden rail fence and continue along the canal through a gravel parking and picnic area.

- Cross Route 96 when you reach East Street.

- Enter the woods immediately behind the East Street road sign, on a white-blazed trail.

- A blue trail heads off to the right. It's a very short loop to the Cartersville site, which you can take to extend your ride. Otherwise, continue straight.

- The trail turns left and follows a chain-link fence back to the parking lot.

Date Enjoyed: _____

Notes:

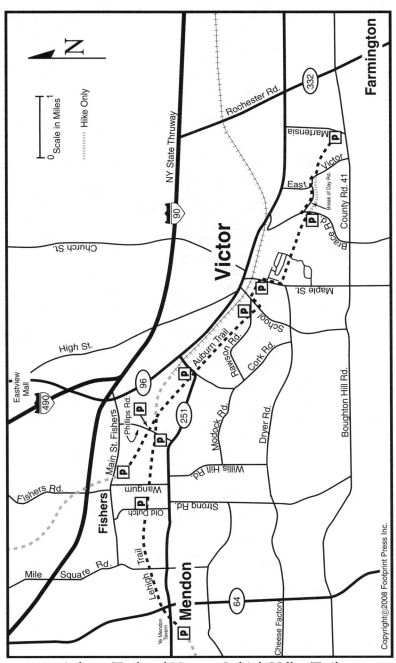

Auburn Trail and Victor - Lehigh Valley Trail

23.
Auburn Trail

Location:	Main Street, Fishers, to Martensia Road in Farmington, Ontario County
Parking:	From Route 96 just south of the I-90 bridge, turn west onto Main Street Fishers. In the village of Fishers turn left into the Fishers Firehouse, and park behind the firehouse.
Alternative Parking:	2-car parking area north of trail on Phillips Road. 2-car parking area north of trail on Route 251. 2-car parking area north of trail on Rawson Road. Victor Volunteer Fireman's Memorial Field on Maple Street in Victor. West side of Martensia Road at brown sign saying "Farmington - Welcome to Auburn Trail."
Riding Time:	65 minutes one way
Length:	6.9 miles one way
Difficulty:	Easy, mostly level
Surface:	Cinder and stone dust trail; some paved trail and road sections
Trail Markings:	3.5-inch white, rectangular, metal markers for "Victor Hiking Trail"
	11-inch green-and-yellow "Victor Hiking Trails" signs at road crossings
	Brown signs for "Farmington - Welcome to Auburn Trail"
Uses:	
Facilities:	None
Dogs:	OK on leash
Admission:	Free

Auburn Trail

Contact: Victor Hiking Trails, Inc.
85 East Main Street, Victor, NY 14564
www.victorhikingtrails.org
hotline: (585) 234-8226

The Auburn Trail was one of the first trails opened by Victor Hiking Trails. This volunteer group was conceived by the Victor Conservation Board in the 1980s. The first organizational meeting occurred in September 1991, and the Auburn Trail opened in September 1993. The eastern section of the Auburn Trail was developed and is maintained by the town of Farmington.

The Auburn Trail is on the bed of the Auburn and Rochester Railroad, which opened in 1840. Charles Fisher owned over 1,000 acres of land in this area and operated a sawmill. "He donated a right-of-way for the railroad through his land. In exchange, he got an agreement that trains would stop at Fishers twice a day, that he would be the station agent, and that he would have the contract for supplying the railroad's lumber needs," per his great-grandson J. Sheldon Fisher in a dedication speech for Lehigh Crossing Park in 2001. At one time, the Auburn was part of the New York Central Railroad System, owned by Cornelius Vanderbilt, and it was the main east-west line in New York State.

Where the Auburn rail bed is not accessible in the village of Victor, this bikeway detours for a short distance on the old Rochester and Eastern Trolley bed. On your journey, you'll pass a train station from each of these lines. The trolley station will be directly in front of you as you cross Maple Street. The former Auburn trail station is in the Whistle Stop Arcade.

At another point two former railroads cross, so you will ride under an old railroad trestle which was used by the Lehigh Valley Railroad. The trestle is now part of the Lehigh Valley Trail. A connector trail was built in 2005 to link the two trails.

If you were to head north from Main Street Fishers, you'd pass through a massive tunnel built large enough for trains, under the New York State Thruway. Unfortunately, a short distance past that, a bridge is being eroded by Irondequoit Creek and is currently dangerous. Victor Hiking

Entering the tunnel under the New York State Thruway.

Trails has plans to rebuild the bridge (very expensive) and extend the Auburn Trail north to Pittsford some time in the future.

Nature is plentiful along the way. Part of the rail bed is raised to overlook beautiful swamp and pond areas. Look carefully as you pedal, and you may be able to pick some blackberries for a quick snack. The trail abounds with birds, beaver, deer, and muskrats.

History will also surround you. Be sure to watch for the old potato storage building and old rail sidings as you pass through Fishers. Stop to admire the cobblestone railroad pump house, built in 1845 (adjacent to the Fishers firehouse). It once pumped water from the creek to fuel the steam-powered locomotives and is the oldest cobblestone railroad building in the country (despite what the sign on its front says). To learn more about the unique cobblestone buildings in this region, pick up a copy of *Cobblestone Quest — Road Tours of New York's Historic Cobblestone Buildings*.

The 1845 cobblestone pump house in the village of Fishers.

Concrete "tombstones" along the way were mileposts for the trains. One marked "S85" denoted that Syracuse was 85 miles away. A "W" in the concrete marker told the engineer that a road crossing was coming and to blow the train's whistle.

Please stay on the white-marked railway bed. Other trails intersect this path, but bikes are not permitted on them.

You'll notice the Lehigh Trail on the map. Like the Auburn Trail, the Lehigh Trail was recently resurfaced and now offers an enjoyable bike ride west to Rush, over the Genesee River and connects to the Genesee Valley Greenway.

Trail Distance Between Major Roads:

Fishers Road to Main Street, Fishers (not included as part of this route)	0.6 mile
Main Street, Fishers to Phillips Road	0.9 mile
Phillips Road to Route 251	1.1 miles
Route 251 to Rawson Road	1.1 miles
Rawson Road to School Street	0.2 mile
School Street to Maple Street	0.6 mile
Maple Street to Whistle Stop	0.4 mile
Whistle Stop to Brace Road	1.2 miles
Brace Road to rail bed on E. Victor Road	0.8 mile
E. Victor Road to Martensia Road	0.6 mile

Trail Directions

• From the Fishers Firehouse, head right on the stone dust trail in front of the cobblestone pump house.
• Notice the old potato storage building on your right. Look for the water ditch from the creek that was used to funnel water to the cobblestone pump house.
• Cross Phillips Road. Parking is available here.
• Ride under the old trestle for the Lehigh Valley Railroad. It was re-decked for pedestrian and bicycle traffic in 2007. (A trail on the right connects the Auburn Trail with the Lehigh Valley Trail.)
• Watch for beaver in the creek to your left.
• Cross Route 251 (Victor-Mendon Road). Parking is available here.

- A red marker for Seneca Trail is on the left. Bikes are not permitted on the Seneca Trail. (See *Take A Hike - Family Walks in the Rochester Area* for details on Seneca Trail.)
- The Seneca Trail (red markers) intersects again.
- Cross Rawson Road. Parking is available here.
- Turn left onto School Street. (The trail ahead turns into Seneca Trail and heads south toward Ganondagan National Historic Site. It is open to walkers only.)
- Just after the post office, the path turns to asphalt.
- Turn right to stay on the asphalt path.
- Cross active railroad tracks, then a wooden bridge.
- Arrive on Maple Street at the Victor Volunteer Fireman's Memorial Field sign. Parking is available here. Directly across Maple Street is the old trolley station, now the offices of Expidata Corporation. Downtown Victor and shops are to the left.
- Turn right (S) on Maple Street. Sidewalks are available on both sides of this busy road.
- Pass stately old homes along Maple Street. Pass East Street.
- Turn left onto the stone dust trail just after the sign for the Whistle Stop Arcade, passing a kiosk and bike rack. The former Rochester and Auburn train station and old railroad cars are on your left.
- Cross Ketchum Road. Ride through a wooded area.
- Victor Hills Golf Course is on the right.
- Turn left onto Brace Road. (The trail ahead, between Brace and East Victor Roads, is a narrow path through close trees. Bikes are not allowed.)
- At the stop sign, turn right onto Break Of Day Road.
- Turn right onto East Victor Road, and head uphill.
- Watch for a yellow-and-green "Hiking Trail" sign on the left, just before the power lines that cross East Victor Road, and turn left onto the trail bed. This section of trail was graded and resurfaced in 2007.
- Pass a brown sign saying "Farmington - Welcome to Auburn Trail."
- Cross a bridge with chain-link sides over Mud Creek. (Notice the gorgeous view of the rock strewn creek to your right. In the spring, look for bluebells.)

- A cement pillar "S82" is hidden in the brush on the right (S) side of the trail. This told the train engineer that it was 82 miles to Syracuse.
- The trail ends at Martensia Road with parking available.

Date Enjoyed: _____

Notes:

24.
Victor - Lehigh Valley Trail

Location: Phillips Road in Victor to the village of Mendon (see map on page 139), Ontario County

Parking: Along Phillips Road. Make sure that you park at the trail crossing closest to Victor-Mendon Road (across from Sealand Contractors). The trail crossing to the north is the Auburn Trail.

Alternative Parking: At the Honeoye Falls—Mendon Youth Baseball Field on Route 251 west of the four corners in Mendon (across from Ye Mendon Tavern)

Riding Time: 30 minutes one way

Length: 2.8 miles one way

Difficulty: Easy, mostly level

Surface: Hard-packed stone dust trail

Trail Markings: 11-inch green-and-yellow "Victor Hiking Trails" signs at road crossings

Uses:

Facilities: Picnic pavilion and Porta-Potties at Mendon Baseball Field, restaurants in Victor

Dogs: OK on leash

Admission: Free

Contact: Victor Hiking Trails, Inc.
85 East Main Street, Victor, NY 14564
www.victorhikingtrails.org
hotline: (585) 234-8226

The Victor - Lehigh Valley Trail used to be deep in ballast stone, but in the winter of 1997, the Victor Department of Transportation graded the path to plow away most of the ballast. Then in 2004/2005 a major project was undertaken to grade and resurface the trail.

The easternmost end connects with the Auburn Trail (#23) where the Lehigh Railroad trestle passes high over the Auburn line. An inclined connector trail was built in 2006 and the trestle was redecked for bikes and pedestrians in 2007. The Lehigh Trail continues east until it meets an active rail line shortly before Route 251. At its western end, it continues past the village of Mendon for 12.5 miles, to cross the Genesee River and meet the Genesee Valley Greenway Trail, as the Mendon - Lehigh Valley Trail (#25).

The Lehigh Valley Railroad got its start in the coal mines of Pennsylvania. Valleys cut by the Lehigh River became channels for transporting the inexpensive, high-grade, anthracite or hard coal from the mines to Rochester and Buffalo. The Rochester station still stands on Court Street across from the Rundel Library. It's now the Dinosaur Bar-B-Que restaurant.

The Lehigh Valley Railroad was built in 1891 to capture some of the lucrative "black diamond" (as coal was nicknamed) freight business. The train, dubbed the "Black Diamond Express," was advertised as the "Handsomest Train in the World." In 1896 it began passenger service between Buffalo and New York. This plush train offered smoking rooms, a polished mahogany library, velvet upholstery, and beveled French-plate mirrors. The engine was an iron horse manufactured by Baldwin. It could reach speeds of 80 miles per hour and maintained its schedule 92% of the time. Honeymooners often rode in luxury to Niagara Falls.

In the 1920s anthracite coal began to lose favor as a home-heating fuel. Homeowners discovered the ease and low cost of gas and oil. By the 1930s the Depression and competition from cars and trucks steadily pulled business away from the trains. Ownership of the rail line changed several times until 1974 when the business was dismantled for scrap iron and parts.

Distance Between Major Roads:

Phillips Road to Wangum Road	0.7 mile
Wangum Road to Old Dutch Road	0.6 mile

Old Dutch Road to Mile Square Road	0.6 mile
Mile Square Road to Route 64	0.6 mile
Route 64 to Route 251	0.2 mile

Trail Directions
- From Phillips Road head west on the trail.
- Pass two paths on the left that lead to a gravel pit.
- Cross Wangum Road (County Road 42), former site of Fisherville.
- A path on the right leads to parking for a local business.
- Cross Old Dutch Road.
- Cross Mile Square Road.
- Ride across a bridge over Irondequoit Creek at 2.5 miles.
- Cross Route 64.
- Cross a small creek.
- Cross Route 251. Parking is available here. The trail continues west to cross the Genesee River and meet the Genesee Valley Greenway Trail. See the Mendon - Lehigh Valley Trail (trail #25, page 150).

Date Enjoyed: _____

Notes:

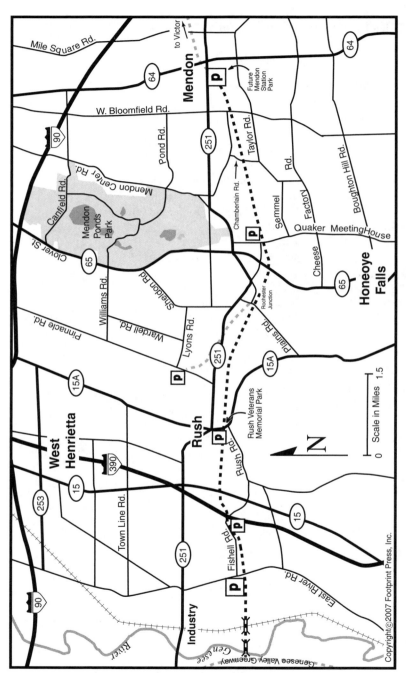

Mendon - Lehigh Valley Trail

25.
Mendon - Lehigh Valley Trail

Location:	Mendon to the Genesee River, Monroe County
Parking:	At the Honeoye Falls—Mendon Youth Baseball Field on Route 251, just west of the four corners of Mendon (across from Ye Mendon Tavern)
Alternative Parking:	East side of Quaker Meeting House Road
	Rush Veterans Memorial Park, Route 15A, Rush
	Behind Rush Creekside Inn, off Route 15A
	Honeoye Creek Fishing Access, Fishell Road, under Interstate 390
	East River Road, south of Fishell Road, Rush
Riding Time:	1 hour and 45 minutes one way
Length:	12.4 miles one way
Difficulty:	Easy, mostly level
Surface:	Hard-packed stone dust trail
Trail Markings:	White signs stating "Motorized Vehicles Prohibited" and white, black and green "Lehigh Valley Trail" signs on posts
Uses:	
Facilities:	Picnic pavilion and Porta-Potties at Mendon Baseball Fields on Route 251 and picnic tables in Rush, restaurants in Mendon & Rush
Dogs:	OK on leash
Admission:	Free
Contact:	The Mendon Foundation P.O. Box 231, Mendon, NY 14506
	Monroe County Parks Department 171 Reservoir Avenue, Rochester, NY 14620 (585) 256-4950

Town of Henrietta, Parks Department
475 Calkins Road, Henrietta, NY 14467
(585) 359-7073

The Lehigh Valley Trail is now a prime biking trail. The Mendon Foundation and Monroe County Parks worked together to turn a once rugged path through the woods into a 10-foot-wide hard surface trail made with compacted, recycled asphalt millings, and a parallel 5-foot-wide grass trail for horseback riding. Six bridges were refurbished, including the bridge that spans the Genesee River and connects this trail to the Genesee Valley Greenway. (The Genesee Valley Greenway in a north/south trail that runs from Genesee Valley Park in Rochester to Cuba. 52 of its planned 90 miles are currently open.)

Don't pass up this ride if you want country solitude through woods and fields, because this path offers it in abundance. It provides a welcome escape from the clutter and noise of urban Rochester.

See page 148 for a short history of the Lehigh Valley Railroad. Rochester Junction in Mendon was a major intersection where trains ran west to Buffalo, south to Hemlock Lake, and north to Rochester. Remains of the old rail station platform are visible today. Plans are developing to build Mendon Station Park at this spot. It will contain pavilions, a history museum, a livery stable, railroad displays, an ice skating rink, and a replica of the former Mendon Station to house restrooms and a warming hut.

As you ride this trail, think back to the times when steam locomotives hauled coal, and the "Black Diamond" transported passengers in luxury. Keep your eyes to the ground, and you may be lucky enough to find a piece of "black diamond" from a bygone era.

At the eastern end, this trail ends in Victor. Connect the route described here with the Victor - Lehigh Valley Trail (#24) for a 15.3 mile adventure (one way).

Riding past a sign for the Lehigh Valley Trail,
before the trail was graded and resurfaced.

Distance Between Parking Areas:

Route 251 to Quaker Meeting House Road	3.6 miles
Quaker Meeting House Road to Route 15A	4.5 miles
Route 15A to Fishell Road	1.8 miles
Fishell Road to East River Road	1.2 miles
East River Road to Genesee River	1.3 miles

Trail Directions
• From the Route 251 parking lot, head southwest past wooden posts.
• Cross a small cement bridge over a creek.
• Cross West Bloomfield Road.
• Parallel Irondequoit Creek on your left for a short while.
• Cross Chamberlain Road at 1.8 miles.
• Cross Quaker Meeting House Road at 3.6 miles.
• Cross Route 65. (Parking is not available at Route 65.)

153

A redecked bridge over Honeoye Creek.
This photo is of the trail before grading and resurfacing.

- On the right pass an old cement platform and switching mechanism. This area was once Rochester Junction where the Lehigh and Conrail trains crossed.
- Cross Plains Road. (Junction Road is visible to the north.)
  Side Trip: In the side yard of the white house (275 Plains Road) another railroad bed heads northwest for 1.9 miles to a parking area along Pinnacle Road. The trail has some rocky spots but is bikable. Henrietta has plans to extend this trail north to Lehigh Station Road.
- Cross over a large metal trestle bridge spanning Honeoye Creek. This bridge has decking and railings spanning 160 feet, compliments of Boy Scout Troop 45 of Rochester, The Monroe County Parks Department, and Mendon Foundation volunteers.
- Emerge onto Park Lane. Honeoye Creek is on your right. There is a picnic area at Rush Veterans Memorial Park.
- Cross Route 15A next to Rush Creekside Inn. You've come 8 miles so far.
- Cross a second trestle bridge over Honeoye Creek.
- Ride under the Route 15 bridge at 9.2 miles.

- The trail bends left, parallel to Interstate 390.
- Head downhill to Fishell Road.
- Turn right and ride under Interstate 390, past Honeoye Creek Fishing Access.
- Shortly after the Interstate 390 bridge, bear left and head uphill on the trail.
- Cross a driveway.
- Cross East River Road at 11.1 miles. This is the last parking area along the trail.
- Cross a bridge over the Conrail tracks.
- Cross a bridge over a swamp.
- Pass a large stone abutment. A large trestle used to span from this point over the Genesee River.
- Cross the Genesee River on the bridge. You're riding on a lower level of the bridge. Trains used to rumble far above your head, across the top of this bridge.
- The Lehigh Valley Trail will meet the north/south Genesee Valley Greenway Trail. From here, you can ride north into Rochester or south to Cuba (with some road sections).

Date Enjoyed: _____

Notes:

Biking is easy on the newly graded and resurfaced
Lehigh Valley Trail.

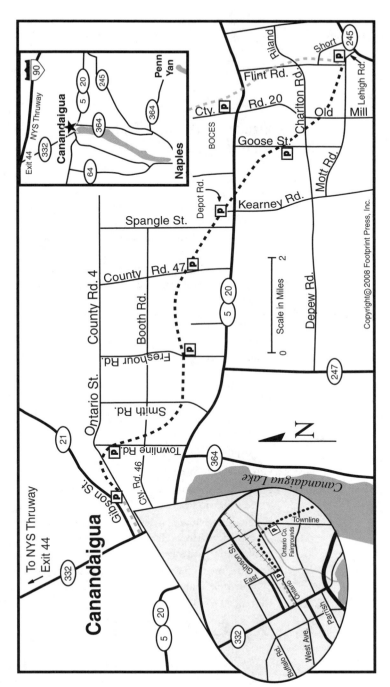

Ontario Pathways Trail - Canandaigua to Stanley

26.
Ontario Pathways Trail
(Canandaigua to Stanley)

Location:	Canandaigua to Stanley, Ontario County
Parking:	From Route 332 in downtown Canandaigua, turn left (E) onto Ontario Street just after the Ontario County Courthouse (a yellow building with a statue on its gold-domed roof). Pass the Ontario County Sheriff and Jail building. Cross active railroad tracks. The parking lot is on the left in front of an old red warehouse.
Alternative Parking:	On Townline Road (County Road 10) near Ontario County Fairgrounds Freshour Road County Road 47 Depot Road Goose Street Mott Road
Riding Time:	2 hours one way
Length:	10.7 miles one way
Difficulty:	Easy, mostly level, some soft grass
Surface:	Cinder and mowed grass
Trail Markings:	Plastic, green-and-white signs that read "Welcome to Ontario Pathways" Green-and-yellow plastic signs that read "Warning No Motorized Vehicles, No Hunting on Trail, Ontario Pathways, Inc." Some segments have numbered wooden posts as half-mile markers Red metal gates at each road crossing
Uses:	

Facilities:	None
Dogs:	OK on leash
Admission:	Free
Contact:	Ontario Pathways
	P.O. Box 996, Canandaigua, NY 14424
	(585) 234-7722
	www.ontariopathways.org

Ontario Pathways is a grass-roots organization, formed in 1993, by people dedicated to the establishment of public-access trails throughout Ontario County. They purchased and are working to develop two rail beds abandoned by the Penn Central Corporation. Trains last thundered over this land in 1972, when Hurricane Agnes hit and damaged many of the rails. When complete, these two rail beds will cover 22 miles from Canandaigua southwest to Stanley, and from Stanley north to Phelps. The segment from Canandaigua to Stanley is complete. A gap remains on the Stanley to Phelps leg (see page 163) which requires a road detour on Wheat Road in Phelps to get around some private property.

The rail bed you'll be riding started operation in 1851, as the Canandaigua Corning Line and was financed by prominent Canandaigua residents Mark Sibley, John Granger, Oliver Phelps III, and Jared Wilson. This short line, like many of its cousins, suffered grave financial losses and changed names four times in 14 years. Even the federal government became involved when, in 1862, President Abraham Lincoln authorized the expenditure of $50,000 to revive the line so that men and supplies could be moved southward to the Civil War battlefront in Pennsylvania. Recruits rode this line to training centers in Elmira, New York, and Harrisburg, Pennsylvania.

By 1880, Canandaigua became a tourist attraction. Cargo switched from agricultural goods to passengers, as five trains ran daily between Canandaigua and Elmira. However, as with all of the railroads, business faded in the 1950s and 1960s because of competition from cars and trucks. The rail line changed hands many more times, until the merger of Northern Central with New York Central to form the Penn Central in 1968. Penn Central filed for bankruptcy in 1970, and train traffic

Pedaling under a colorful fall canopy
on the Ontario Pathways Trail.

dwindled even further. When Hurricane Agnes blew through the area in 1972, she damaged bridges, tracks, and rail beds. Penn Central abandoned the line, sold the rails for scrap, and sold the land corridor in 1994 to Ontario Pathways.

The trail is a 10-foot-wide swath through lush countryside. We rode it in the fall, pedaling over a bed of colored leaves with the canopy above blazing reds and yellows. It would be a delight to ride this trail in any season except, of course, the snow season when cross-country skis or snowshoes would be more appropriate.

Trail Distance Between Major Roads:
Canandaigua Downtown Spur
Route 332 to Ontario Street   0.4 mile
Ontario Street to East Street   0.5 mile
From 1st Parking Lot
East Street to Ontario Street   0.9 mile
Ontario Street to County Road 10 (Townline Road) 0.4 mile

County Road 10 to County Road 46	0.8 mile
County Road 46 to Smith Road	1.0 mile
Smith Road to Freshour Road	0.9 mile
Freshour Road to County Road 47	1.6 mile
County Road 47, past Spangle to Depot Road	1.7 mile
Depot Road, past Route 5&20 to Goose Street	1.8 mile
Goose Street to Depew/Charlton Road	0.4 mile
Depew/Charlton Road to Old Mill Road	0.5 mile
Old Mill Road to Mott Road	0.7 mile

Trail Directions
From Canandaigua:
- From the parking area on Ontario Street head northeast on the trail, away from the city of Canandaigua, parallel to an active set of railroad tracks. If you're lucky, a train will come by.
- Cross East Street.
- Pass a red metal gate. On the left, watch for the cement pillar with "S73" denoting 73 miles to Syracuse.
- After a while, the trail and railroad tracks diverge.
- Head downhill past a red gate. Cross Ontario Street.
- Head uphill, then cross a long wooden bridge over Canandaigua Outlet.
- The Ontario County Fair Grounds appear on your right.
- Cross Townline Road (County Road 10) near the entrance to the Fair Grounds.
- Cross County Road 46. You've now come 2.4 miles.
- Cross a dirt driveway.
- Cross Smith Road. Then cross several farm lanes.
- Pass a red metal gate, then a farm lane.
- Pass another farm lane, buildings, and a sheep pasture on the left. Continue straight on the trail, passing a farm pond and a farm lane to the right.
- At 5.9 miles, cross County Road 47. Pass a metal gate.
- Cross several farm lanes.
- Pass a red metal gate, cross Spangle Road, then pass another gate.
- Bear right heading downhill. Cross a farm lane that goes past old railroad abutments, then head uphill back to the railroad bed.

- You'll see houses on the right and the end of Depot Road where parking is available. You've come 7.6 miles.
- Cross a farm lane, then pass a metal gate.
- Cross over Routes 5 & 20 on a railroad bridge.
- The trail dips at a farm lane then crosses a small bridge.
- Cross more farm lanes.
- Pass a metal gate just before crossing Goose Street at 9.4 miles.
- Cross Depew/Charlton Road.
- Cross a long bridge.
- Cross Old Mill Road at 10.3 miles.
- Cross Flint Road.
- Soon, reach the gravel parking area tucked between Mott and Lehigh Roads. (To continue on the trail, take an immediate left before the parking area, heading north. See page163.)

Date Enjoyed: _____

Notes:

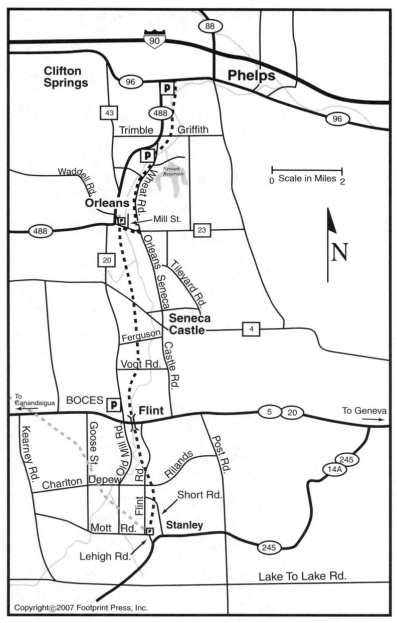

Ontario Pathways Trail - Stanley to Phelps

27.
Ontario Pathways Trail
(Stanley to Phelps)

Location:	Stanley to Phelps, Ontario County
Parking:	From Route 245 in Stanley (south of Routes 5 & 20), turn north on Lehigh Road. The parking area is at the first sharp bend where Lehigh Road turns into Mott Road.
Alternative Parking:	Off Waddell Road, at the corner of County Road 23
	Along the edge of Wheat Road (except from November through April)
	On the south side of Route 96 east of the Route 488 intersection in Phelps
Riding Time:	1.5 hours one way
Length:	9.5 miles one way
Difficulty:	Easy, mostly level
Surface:	Cinder and mowed grass, paved roads
Trail Markings:	Plastic, green-and-white signs that read "Welcome to Ontario Pathways"
	Green-and-yellow plastic signs that read "Warning No Motorized Vehicles, No Hunting on Trail, Ontario Pathways, Inc."
Uses:	
Facilities:	None
Dogs:	OK on leash
Admission:	Free
Contact:	Ontario Pathways P.O. Box 996, Canandaigua, NY 14424 (585) 234-7722 www.ontariopathways.org

The old water tower in Orleans.

This is a continuation of Ontario Pathways Trail, see page 157. To ride from Stanley to Phelps requires a 2.2-mile road ride between trail segments. Much of this trail is new and therefore less travelled, making it a softer, grassy path ride. Watch for woodchuck holes as you ride. Ontario Pathways volunteers attempt to keep the holes filled but woodchucks are an ambitious lot. The path is covered by a cooling tree canopy and has a more intimate feel than the segment toward Canandaigua.

Distance Between Major Roads (Stanley to Phelps):

Mott Road to Short Road	0.6 mile
Short Road to Rilands Road	0.3 mile
Rilands Road to Vogt Road (crossing over Routes 5& 20 on a new bridge)	2.5 miles
Vogt Road to Ferguson Road	0.4 mile
Ferguson Road to County Road 4	0.5 mile
County Road 4 to County Road 23	1.3 mile
Road segment (Waddell Road to Wheat Road)	2.2 miles
Wheat Road to Trimble Griffith Road	0.5 mile
Trimble Griffith Road to Route 96	1.2 miles

Trail Directions

- From the parking area, take a right, heading north.
- Cross Short Road, then Rilands Road.
- Cross Flint Road.
- The trail will cross over Routes 5 & 20 on a bridge that was rebuilt in 2007.
- Cross 2 small bridges then pass a gate.
- Cross ATV paths and reach Vogt Road at 3.4 miles.
- Cross Ferguson Road, then in another 0.5 mile, cross County Road 4.
- Ride over a creek on an earthen embankment.
- Cross over a pipeline.
- Flint Creek comes and goes from view far below. In spots you'll ride close to a precipitous ledge.
- Reach County Road 23 at 5.6 miles. (A large parking area and a wood-shingled water tower are at this corner.)

Approaching a gate on a stretch of Ontario Pathways Trail.

- Turn right on County Road 23 to begin the 2.2-mile road section. Cross Flint Creek and pass Mill Street.
- Turn left onto Wheat Road, heading north.
- Pass roads to the left then right.
- Cross Flint Creek.
- Turn right to pick up the Ontario Pathways Trail (just south of the Route 488 junction).
- Cross Griffith Road.
- Cross a small wooden bridge.
- Cross Flint Creek. Notice the waterfalls to your right.
- Pass old railroad bridge abutments.
- Rest at the bench.
- Cross Flint Creek again.
- Reach the Route 96 parking area.

Date Enjoyed: _____
Notes:

The new Ontario Pathways bridge over
Routes 5 & 20 in Flint.

Rides South
of Rochester

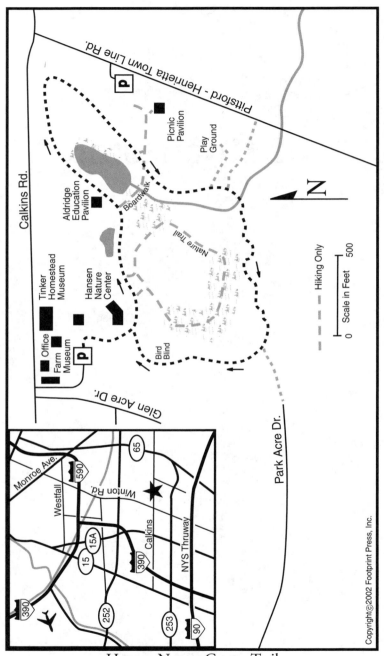

Hansen Nature Center Trail

28.
Hansen Nature Center Trail

Location:	Henrietta (between Pinnacle Road and Henrietta-Pittsford Townline Road), Monroe County
Parking:	Parking lot at Hansen Nature Center, 1525 Calkins Road
Riding Time:	20-minute loop
Length:	1.2-mile loop
Difficulty:	Easy, mostly level
Surface:	Stone dust path
Trail Markings:	None
Uses:	
Facilities:	Restrooms in nature center, picnic pavilion, playground, FitTrail™ exercise stations
Dogs:	Pets are NOT allowed
Admission:	Free
Contact:	Hansen Nature Center 1525 Calkins Road P.O. Box 999, Henrietta, NY 14467-0999 (585) 359-7044 http://hansennaturecenter.googlepages.com
	Tinker Museum (585) 359-7042

Donated by the Aldridge family in 1991 and made public in 1994, Tinker Nature Park has become a year-round favorite for all ages. The park consists of woods, wetlands, ponds, and fields, which together create a living museum of natural history. Within the park is the Hansen Nature Center, offering classes in cross-country skiing, snowshoeing, photography, wildflowers, songbirds, etc. While there, visit the Tinker Homestead built in 1830. This cobblestone museum is free and open to

A goose makes its home in the wetlands in Tinker Nature Park.

the public on Tuesday, Wednesday, Thursday, Saturday, and Sunday from 11 AM to 3 PM. It can be opened for groups and at other times by appointment.

The biking trail (Perimeter Trail) is a wide, stone dust trail that's easy to bike and suitable for small children.

Trail Directions
• From the parking lot follow the brick path, bearing left past the nature center.
• Continue straight on the stone dust path. (Trail to the right is a board-walk that is for hikers   only.)
• Continue following the stone dust path past a pavilion and picnic area. (The boardwalk shortcut rejoins the Perimeter Trail.)
• Bear right past the Pittsford-Henrietta Town Line Road parking area.
• Pass a boardwalk path on the right and the playground on the left.

- Pass a side trail to Pittsford-Henrietta Town Line Road.
- Pass a side trail to Park Acre Drive.
- Wind through woods reemerging in a meadow near the nature center.
- Turn left to follow the brick path back to the parking lot.

Date Enjoyed: _____

Notes:

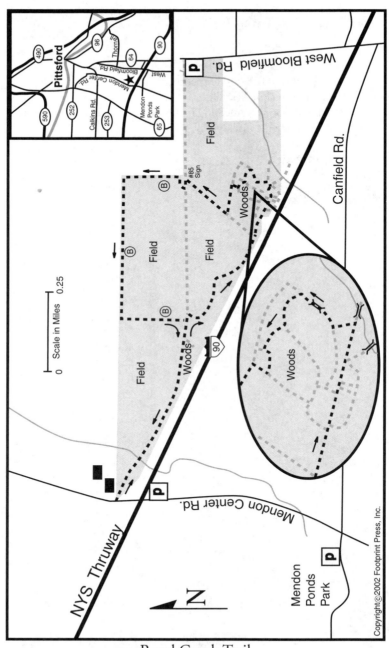

Royal Coach Trail

Copyright:©2002 Footprint Press, Inc.

Scale in Miles
0   0.25

N

NYS Thruway

Mendon Center Rd.

West Bloomfield Rd.

Canfield Rd.

Field

Field

Field

Field

Field

Woods

Woods

Woods

Mendon
Ponds
Park

P

P

P

90

#85
Sign

B

B

B

490

Pittsford

96

Thornell

590

252

253

65

64

90

Mendon Center Rd.

West
Bloomfield Rd.

Calkins Rd.

Mendon
Ponds
Park

29.
Royal Coach Trail

Location:	Mendon Center Road, Pittsford, Monroe County
Directions:	From Pittsford, head south on Route 64. Bear right onto Mendon Center Road. Parking is not allowed at the trailhead. Park along Mendon Center Road just south of the NYS Thruway overpass.
Alternative Parking:	Along Canfield Road in Mendon Ponds Park
	A gravel pull-off area along West Bloomfield Road
Biking Time:	30-minute loop
Length:	2.2-mile loop
Difficulty:	Difficult, rough mountain bike trail
Surface:	Mowed-grass and dirt trails
Trail Markings:	Blue blazes on part of the loop
Uses:	
Facilities:	None
Dogs:	OK on leash
Admission:	Free
Contact:	Pittsford Parks & Recreation
	35 Lincoln Avenue, Pittsford, NY 14534
	(585) 248-6280

Royal Coach gets its name from Walnut Hill Farms which abuts the property on the eastern edge. Each August, Walnut Hill is the meeting place for elaborate horse drawn coaches and carts. They host a competition of driving skill and give awards for costuming and restoration of the old carriages. Watching the competition is a fun way to spend a summer day. The horses and carts use the trails through the woods at the eastern end of this property for their time trials.

175

On a fall day, while biking on Royal Coach Trail, we were treated to a rare sight. A young gray fox pranced in front of us and pounced several times as he hunted for mice in the fields. We were down wind so it was only when we crept forward to get a better look that he took note of us and bounded away.

The trail begins with a climb past farm fields. Once at the top of the hill you enter a maze of trails in a deep woods. This is where the driving competition takes place. A sculptor has been busy in the area. On our last ride here, the woods had sprouted a fox and a pine tree carved into the trunks of downed trees. The return winds downhill around fields.

The drone of Thruway noise is never out of earshot but the splendor of hilltop vistas makes it bearable. In fall, the reds, bronzes, yellows, and greens of the trees contrast sharply with the beige carpet of dying corn-stalks. This is indeed a pretty, if challenging place to go for a ride.

Trail Directions
- Follow Mendon Center Road north, passing under the NYS Thruway bridge.
- Less than 0.1 mile from the Thruway bridge, turn right (E) at the green "Town of Pittsford Parkland Restrictions" sign.
- Ride east on a farm lane. It parallels the Thruway and heads uphill.
- At 0.3 mile a woods begins to your right.
- Pass a mowed trail to the left (this will be your return loop).
- Turn right at 0.4 mile and follow the mowed-grass trail around the edge of a field toward the Thruway. (You're on an unmarked trail.)
- Parallel the Thruway then proceed straight (E).
- Pass a grassy trail to the left and continue straight (E) entering the woods at 0.7 mile. (The woods are full of many intersecting trails.)
- Continue straight on the wide path. (You'll pass a trail to the left, then a trail to the right marked with a "Camper's Path" sign.)
- Keep going straight. (You'll pass a trail on the left then 3 trails to the right. The third right leads over a small bridge.)
- At 0.8 mile turn left (N) and head uphill toward a wooden cut-out of a leaning man. (If you miss this turn you'll cross a bridge over a small creek. This is private property, so turn around.)

- Reach a "Y" and turn right (NE).
- Cross a wooden bridge then bear left to stay in the woods. (Straight leads to a field.)
- At 0.9 mile, bear right (N) and pass a fox carved from a tree on your left.
- Bear left and follow the trail as it winds through the woods. (Right leads to a field.)
- At the pine tree carving, turn right (N) and enter the field.
- At the end of the field, turn left and follow the edge of the field (NW).
- At 1.1 miles, reach a wide "T" and turn right (NE) on a wide grass strip between fields.
- Reach a "T" and gas line post #85. Turn left (NW). (Right leads to West Bloomfield Road.)
- Quickly turn right (N) on the blue-blazed trail. (The trail winds through wooded hedge rows.)
- Bear left twice, following the blue blazes around the perimeter of a field, then head downhill. Watch for wood chuck holes.
- At 1.6 miles, bear left again then head uphill.
- Reach a wide mowed "T" at 1.7 miles and turn right (NW) between the woods and a field.
- Follow the farm road back down to Mendon Center Road.
- Turn left to return to your car.

Date Enjoyed: _____

Notes:

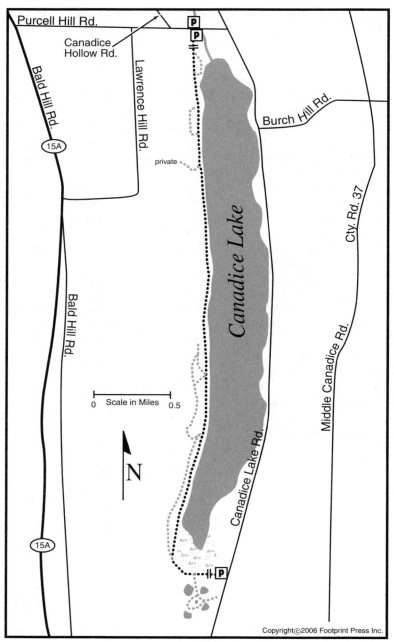

Canadice Lake Trails

30.
Canadice Lake Trail

Location:	West side of Canadice Lake, Ontario County
Parking:	From Route 15A, turn east onto Purcell Hill Road. Find a dirt parking area on the north side, mid way between Canadice Hollow Road and Canadice Lake Road. Additional parking is available at the beginning of the trail.
Alternative Parking:	A small pull-off along Canadice Lake Road, 3.7 miles south of Purcell Hill Road on west side of road (lake side), near a blue gate.
Riding Time:	70 minutes round trip
Length:	8.1 miles round trip
Difficulty:	Easy, mostly level on the trail parallel to the lake. The loops up the hillside require technical mountain biking and are not currently well marked.
Surface:	Gravel and grass double-track
Trail Markings:	Green-and-white signs labeled with hiker silhouettes and "Hemlock Canadice Watershed"
Uses:	
Facilities:	None
Dogs:	OK on leash
Admission:	Free, but pick up a permit
Contact:	City of Rochester, Water and Lighting Bureau 7412 Rix Hill Road, Hemlock, NY 14466 (585) 428-3646

Early settlers tried to farm around Canadice Lake but found the glacially scoured land ill-suited for farming. Many areas around the lake were too steep or too wet for growing crops. Eventually, the Canadice Lake shore became rimmed with cottages. However, in 1872 the city of Rochester decided to use Canadice and Hemlock Lakes as a water supply. The first conduit for water was completed in 1876. By 1947 Rochester had purchased all of the shoreline property and removed the cottages in order to help protect the water supply for its growing population. Although it was very difficult for the cottage residents to leave their land, this area is now free of the commercialization that is so rampant on the other Finger Lakes. Ninety-foot-deep Canadice Lake is the smallest of the Finger Lakes, but it has the highest elevation, at 1,096 feet, one of the reasons it is such a good water supply for the city. Flow from Canadice Outlet Creek is diverted into the northern end of Hemlock Lake. From there the City of Rochester Water Bureau conditions the water for drinking and uses gravity to send it north for 29 miles via large pipes at a rate of up to 48 million gallons per 24-hour period.

Today, the Hemlock and Canadice Lakes watershed continues to be Rochester's primary source of drinking water. The watershed covers more

The serene Canadice Lake Trail.

than 40,000 acres of land, of which Rochester owns 7,000 acres. A second-growth forest prospers on the land and many abandoned farm fields have been reforested with conifers. Bald eagles are now present in the area.

To protect city property and the supply of drinking water, the city asks that all visitors obtain a Watershed Visitor Permit, one of the easiest permits to obtain. Just stop at the visitor's self-serve, permit station located at the north end of Hemlock Lake on Rix Hill Road off Route 15A (see the map on page 183) or download it at www.cityofrochester.gov/watershedpermit.htm. There are no fees or forms to fill out, but the permit document details the dos and don'ts to help keep the area pristine, so it's important to read it. Swimming and camping are not permitted. Boats up to 16 feet long with motors up to 10 horsepower are okay.

The Canadice Lake Trail, an abandoned town road, meanders back and forth through oak, maple, tulip poplar, and conifer trees, but is never very far from the lake. See if you can spot the old cottage foundations along the way.

Trail Directions
- From the parking area, head south past the silver gate.
- Pass a side loop to the left (level and easy biking), then multiple trails to your right. (You can bike these, but they are steep dirt paths with sharp bends. Only attempt them with a mountain bike.)
- At the end of the lake, the trail turns left (E) onto gravel.
- At the bench you have a choice. You can continue straight and soon arrive at a blue, gated trail entrance off of Canadice Lake Road or you can turn right to explore a circle trail with a bench in the center. Off the circle is another trail that also takes you to Canadice Lake Road.

Date Enjoyed: _____

Notes:

Rest at this bench to enjoy a view
of the south end of Canadice Lake.

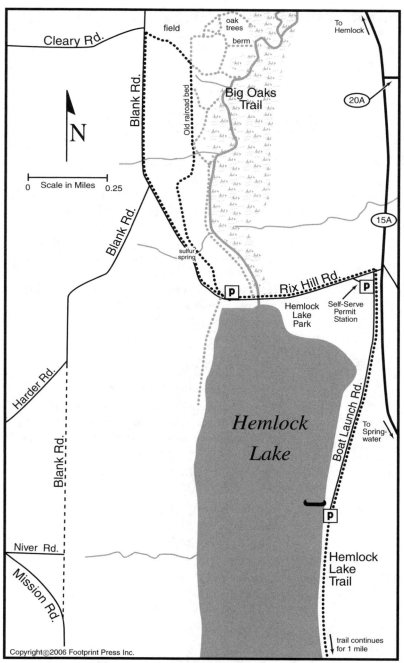

Cleary Rd.

field

oak trees

berm

To Hemlock

Blank Rd.

Old railroad bed

Big Oaks Trail

20A

N

0 Scale in Miles 0.25

15A

sulfur spring

P

Rix Hill Rd.

P

Hemlock Lake Park

Self-Serve Permit Station

Harder Rd.

Hemlock Lake

Boat Launch Rd.

To Spring- water

Blank Rd.

P

Niver Rd.

Hemlock Lake Trail

Mission Rd.

Copyright©2006 Footprint Press Inc.

trail continues for 1 mile

Hemlock Lake & Big Oaks Trails

31.
Hemlock Lake & Big Oak Trails

Location: North end of Hemlock Lake, Livingston and
              Ontario Counties

Parking: From Route 15A at the north end of Hemlock Lake,
              turn west onto Rix Hill Road. Take the first right
              and park in the loop near the self-serve permit area.

Alternative Parking: From the permit area loop, head south on Boat
              Launch Road for 1.1 miles to park at the end,
              near the boat launch.

              From the permit area, drive west on Rix-Hill Road,
              cross Hemlock Lake Outlet and park at the
              trailhead on the right.

Riding Time: 1.5-hour loop

Length: 10.1-mile loop

Difficulty: Easy for the 6 miles parallel to Hemlock Lake
              Moderate for the full loop

Surface: Dirt road, dirt double-track and woodland trails south
              of the permit station, mowed-grass trails (may be
              tall grass, may be wet) on Big Oaks Trail segment

Trail Markings: None

Uses: 🏃 🚴 🏃

Facilities: Portable toilet at boat launch
              Restrooms (May through Mid-October), picnic tables,
              playground in Hemlock Lake Park (7 AM-10 PM)

Dogs: OK on leash

Admission: Free, but pick up a permit

Contact: City of Rochester, Water and Lighting Bureau
              7412 Rix Hill Road, Hemlock, NY 14466
              (585) 428-3646

184

Early settlers tried to farm around Hemlock Lake but found the steep, glacially scoured land ill-suited for farming. In 1872 the city of Rochester decided to use Canadice and Hemlock Lakes as a water supply. The first conduit for water was completed in 1876. By 1947 Rochester had purchased and removed cottages that had been built along the shores in order to help protect the water supply for its growing population. This area is now free of the commercialization that is so rampant on the other Finger Lakes. From Hemlock Lake, the City of Rochester Water Bureau conditions the water for drinking and uses gravity to send it north for 29 miles via large pipes at a rate of up to 48 million gallons per 24-hour period.

Today, the Hemlock and Canadice Lakes watershed continues to be Rochester's primary source of drinking water. The watershed covers more than 40,000 acres of land, of which Rochester owns 7,000 acres. A second-growth forest prospers on the land and many abandoned farm fields have been reforested with conifers. Bald eagles are now present in the area.

To protect city property and the supply of drinking water, the city asks that all visitors obtain a Watershed Visitor Permit, one of the easiest permits to obtain. Just stop at the visitor's self-serve permit station located at the north end of Hemlock Lake on Rix Hill Road off Route 15A, or you can download it at www.cityofrochester.gov/watershed-permit.htm. There are no fees or forms to fill out, but the permit document details the dos and don'ts to help keep the area pristine, so it's important to read it. Swimming and camping are not permitted.

The watershed area contains a variety of trees, including hemlock, beech, oak, maple, hickory, basswood, and white, red and scotch pine. You may see kingfishers, herons, ospreys, as well as bald eagles near the water. The relatively undisturbed forest along the trails is ideal habitat for several woodpecker species. Also, the narrow lake and forested shoreline create excellent sighting opportunities for spring and autumn migrating warblers and other songbirds.

The trail described follows dirt Boat Launch Road, then a double-track dirt trail, packed hard from City of Rochester, Water and Lighting Bureau truck tires to a stone bench with a panoramic view of Hemlock Lake. Then return to the permit station and head west along Rix Hill Road to the grassy Big Oaks Trail for a loop. A portion of the trail follows the former

185

bed of the Lehigh Valley Railroad. Watch for an old foundation near the sulfur spring. Big Oaks Trail heads into a marshy area surrounding Hemlock Lake Outlet and can be very wet in spring. Late summer or fall is the best time to bicycle here.

Trail Directions
- From the self-serve permit stand off Rix Hill Road, begin your southward journey on the paved loop.
- Turn right (S) onto the seasonal dirt road leading to the boat launch.
- Pass the boat launch and portable toilet at 1.1 miles. Continue straight past the grey metal gate.
- At 2.8 miles the double-track ends. Leave your bike here, or walk it over the culvert and onto a narrow path through the woods.
- In another 0.1 mile you'll reach a stone bench overlooking Hemlock Lake, the perfect place for a contemplative break.
- Reverse direction to follow the double-track and seasonal road back to the self-serve permit stand at 5.9 miles.
- Turn left and follow Rix Hill Road.
- Pass the water filtration plant, then the entrance to Hemlock Lake Park at 6.2 miles.
- Cross the bridge over Hemlock Lake Outlet.
- In another 0.1 mile, turn right through the trail parking area and pass a silver metal gate. This is marked with a green-and-white sign that reads "Hemlock-Canadice Watershed."
- You're now on a grass trail (sporadically mowed). Cross two small streams.
- At 7.2 miles (0.7 miles on this trail) the first loop trail heads off to the right. (You can take this 0.25-mile loop if you wish.)
- The return of the side loop trail meets the main trail at 7.4 miles.
- Pass a third trail to the right. (This is the start of a loop through a field.)
- Pass a forth trail to the right. (This is the end of the field loop.)
- Continue along the edge of a field.
- Reach Blank Road at 7.7 miles. Turn left to ride south on Blank Road.
- Bear left onto Rix Hill Road to return to the self-serve permit station.

Date Enjoyed: _____
Notes:

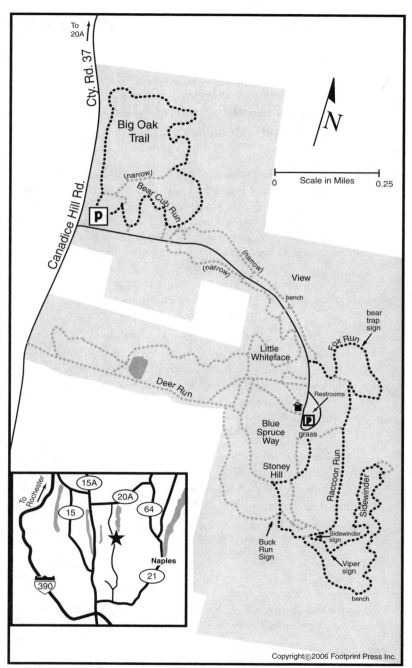

Harriet Hollister Spencer Memorial State Recreation Area

32.
Harriet Hollister Spencer Memorial State Recreation Area

Location:	South of Honeoye Lake, Ontario County
Parking:	From Route 390, head east on Route 20A through Livonia. Continue east past Route 15A. Turn south on Canadice Hill Road (County Road 37). Pass Ross Road. Canadice Hill Road will turn to gravel. Turn left at the sign "Harriet Hollister Spencer Memorial State Recreation Area" and park in the parking area on the left.
Alternative Parking:	Along the loop at the end of the park road.
Length:	Over 10 miles of trails
Difficulty:	Moderate, hilly (mountain biking)
Surface:	Dirt trails
Trail Markings:	Some cross-country ski trail signs (blue squares, black diamonds) and some brown-and-yellow trail name signs
Uses:	
Facilities:	Restroom (in the center of the park road loop), picnic tables
Dogs:	OK on leash
Admission:	Free
Contact:	NYS Office of Parks, Recreation, and Historic Preservation Stony Brook State Park 10820 Route 36 South, Dansville, NY 14437 (585) 335-8111

High in the hills, between Canadice Lake and Honeoye Lake, this area is treasured by cross-country skiers because it often has snow when the surrounding area doesn't. The trails in this park are constructed, maintained, and groomed in winter by volunteers from the N.Y.S. Section 5 Ski League. The rest of the year, the trails are lesser used and are a wonderland for hikers and off-road bikers.

A trail parallel to the park road offers a grand view of Honeoye Lake in the valley. A bench labeled "A favorite place of Todd Ewers" is available to sit and savor the view.

Within the woods you'll follow 8-foot wide, hard-packed dirt trails. Sometimes narrow trails veer off as shortcuts or deer paths, but stay on the wide trails.

Big Oak and Bear Cub Loop
Riding Time: 20 minute loop
Length: 1.9-mile loop (darkened trail)

The Big Oak and Bear Cub Trail loop rambles through deep woods and is shady and cool on a hot day. We once watched a family of baby raccoons play along the trail. The southeast section of this loop is steep.

Trail Directions
•From the parking area near Canadice Hill Road, head north on the trail.
•Bear left on Big Oak Trail past a blue, "more difficult" cross-country ski sign. (Bear Cub Run is to the right.)
•Follow the trail around, staying on the main trail.
•Toward the top of a hill, bear right, then take a quick right turn. You're now on Bear Cub Run. (Straight leads to the park road.)
•At the "T," turn left to return to the parking area.

Date Enjoyed: _____
Notes:

Honeoye Lake as viewed from
Harriet Hollister Spencer Memorial Recreation Area.

Fox Run - Raccoon Run - Sidewinder Loop
Riding Time: 30 minute loop
Length: 2.6-mile loop (darkened trail)

Take a longer ride through these pristine woods by combining several trails. The trails are poorly marked, but a few signs along the way can act as waymarkers.

Trail Directions
• Park along the loop at the end of the park road.
• Ride back down the road to find the first trail to the right (E), labeled Fox Run.
• Follow Fox Run as it winds, passing a "bear trap" sign.
• When the trail meets Raccoon Run, turn left.
• Take the first left onto Sidewinder at the sign "Sidewinder - one way." As the name implies, this trail will wind.
• Pass a "viper" sign.
• Pass a bench at the base of a steep hill.
• At the "T" turn left.
• Continue straight through a trail junction.
• At the next "T," turn right.
• Pass a trail to the right, then one to the left. Follow the trail downhill to a grassy area.
• Cross the grass to return to the parking loop.

Date Enjoyed: _____

Notes:

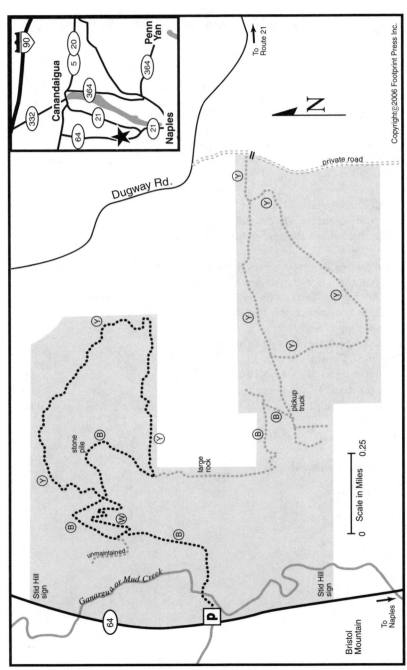

Stid Hill Multiple Use Area

33.
Stid Hill Multiple Use Area

Location: Bristol, Ontario County

Parking: Take Route 64 south from Route 5 & 20. The Stid Hill parking area is 1.7 miles south of Dugway Road (bottom of the hill), just past the D.E.C. "Stid Hill" sign.

Alternative Parking: Along Dugway Road, 2.0 miles from Route 64 (top of the hill), where a square yellow sign on a tree up a steep dirt road reads "Unauthorized Vehicles Prohibited" Below it is a round, yellow D.E.C. marker.

Riding Time: 40 minute loop

Length: 3.4-mile loop (darkened trail)

6.5 miles total trails

Difficulty: Difficult - mountain biking only

Surface: Dirt trail

Trail Markings: 3"round, yellow D.E.C. markers, color blazes

Uses:

Facilities: None

Dogs: OK

Admission: Free, open June 1 through late fall

Contact: New York State D.E.C.
6274 East Avon-Lima Road, Avon, NY 14414
(585) 226-2466

Rochester Bicycling Club
PO Box 10100, Rochester, NY 14610
www.rochesterbicyclingclub.org

Stid Hill, as the name implies, sits on the side of a hill. The area, opposite Bristol Mountain Ski Resort, is comprised of 3 tracts of land totalling 740 acres. At one time, Stid Hill was productive sheep and cattle grazing land. The livestock are gone. Left behind are steep hills, ravines, gullies, gorges, woods, and open fields that provide varied habitat for wildlife.

Included in the wildlife you'll find on Stid Hill are mountain biking enthusiasts. Members of the Rochester Bicycling Club and the National Mountain Bike Patrol created, maintain, and patrol the trails you'll ride. The trails are in great shape, and we thoroughly enjoyed biking here. The trail directions describe a loop starting from and returning to Route 64. For a long downhill run, start off Dugway Road and head down to Route 64.

Because these trails traverse a steep hillside, they are prone to erosion. Please follow these guidelines to assure safety for all and the continued access to the trails by bikers.

- Ride only between June 1st and late fall. May is spring turkey hunting season and hunters have primary access to the area.
- Since this is a game management area, it's best to wear blaze orange during fall hunting season.
- To minimize erosion, ride softly, carry across soft spots, carry across streams, do not widen the trail or weave around obstacles, do not skid or cut across switchbacks.
- We share these lands. Please do not spook the wildlife.

Trail Directions
- From the Route 64 parking area, follow the mowed-grass trail, and cross a bridge over Ganargua Creek.
- At the white trail, turn right to head uphill.
- Continue straight onto the yellow trail.
- At the blue trail, turn right.
- Follow the blue trail downhill, all the way to the parking area.

Date Enjoyed: _____

Notes:

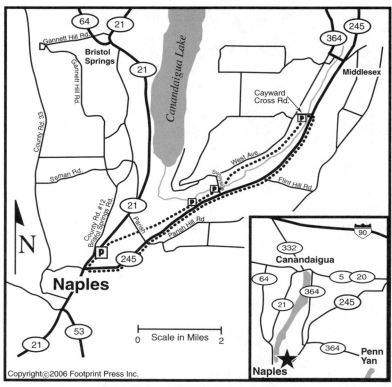

Middlesex Valley Rail Trail

34.
Middlesex Valley Rail Trail

Location:	Hi-Tor area, Naples, Yates County
Parking:	From Route 21, just north of Naples, past the inter section of County Road 12, turn right into a large, dirt, pull-off area.
Alternative Parking:	Route 245, Hi-Tor Management Area - West River Unit (boat launch)
	Sunnyside Road off Route 245, West River Fishing Access
	Trail's endpoint at Cayward Cross Road, off Route 245
Riding Time:	1 hour one way
	If you return on roads, the round trip is 1.6 hours (14.6 miles round trip)
Length:	6.8 miles one way
Difficulty:	Moderate, level with gradual uphill, small section of ballast stone
Surface:	Mowed grass (the mowing may be sporadic, depending on current financing levels at DEC)
Trail Markings:	None
Uses:	
Facilities:	None
Dogs:	OK on leash
Admission:	Free
Contact:	New York State DEC
	6274 Avon-Lima Road, Avon, NY 14414
	(585) 226-2466
	www.dec.state.ny.us

Don't let the fact that this is an old rail bed fool you into thinking it's an easy ride. As you pedal north, you don't notice a grade, but the pedaling is tough as the trail goes steadily uphill. This ride is well worth the effort, however, because you'll find scenery that you won't see on any other rail trail. You'll ride through Middlesex Valley with the towering hills of Naples on both sides.

Most of the rail bed is a raised platform through a wetland. But, because it passes through wetlands, it may be impassable in wet weather.

Along the way are waterfowl nesting boxes, and about one mile south-west of Cayward Cross Road is a blue heron rookery. Please be quiet, and don't disturb the birds.

The official name of this trail is the Lehigh Valley Rail Trail. But since other sections of the Lehigh are open for biking and hiking, we've called it by its historical name. The Middlesex Valley Railroad first provided service between Naples and Stanley in 1892. The line was later extended to Geneva. In 1895 the rail line was purchased by the Lehigh Valley Railroad. Service continued until 1970 when the line was abandoned due to compe-

One of several bridges to cross on the Middlesex Valley Rail Trail.

tition from trucks and cars for the freight of coal, building materials, farm equipment, apples, grapes, beans, etc. Most of the land reverted to private ownership. This portion of the rail trail is owned by New York State as part of the Hi Tor Wildlife Management Area. It is a public hunting ground, so avoid hunting season, or at least wear blaze-orange clothing.

Trail Distance Between Major Roads:

Route 21 to Parish Hill	1.2 miles
Parish Hill to Sunnyside	2.6 miles
Sunnyside to Cayward Cross	3.0 miles

Trail Directions
- Head toward the yellow metal gate and stop sign onto a 12-foot-wide, mowed-grass path.
- Cross the first of many wooden bridges over a creek.
- Emerge from the woods to a vineyard, then a field on your right. The Naples hills tower above as a backdrop to the fields.
- Continue parallel to the creek.
- Cross the second wooden bridge. These bridges were repaired by the NY State Department of Environmental Conservation.
- Pass a yellow metal gate then cross Parish Hill Road.
- Pass another yellow metal gate and ride through a raised bed over wetlands.
- Cross the third wooden bridge. There are some short sections of ballast stone.
- Cross the forth wooden bridge, then a few more short sections of ballast.
- The trail now runs parallel to a road.
- Cross the fifth wooden bridge. You may have to walk your bike. Some of the top planks are rotted.
- Pass through a backyard of farm animals. This is home to a horse, donkey, lamb, and goat as well as many ducks, geese, guinea fowl, turkeys, chickens, and rabbits. The front of this home is a roadside farm stand which sells produce, tarts, pies, breads, snacks, and drinks.
- Pass through another yellow gate into the parking area and boat launch for Hi Tor Management Area — West River Unit.
- Head toward the first yellow gate.

- Pass more yellow gates.
- Pass the West River Fishing Access site. (The West River is on your left. Across the river is the legendary site of the first Seneca Indian village, Nundawao.)
- Cross Sunnyside Road near another West River Fishing Access site. You've ridden 3.8 miles so far.
- Pass yellow gates.
- Cross a long wooden bridge (the 6th) where the waters fork. Trailers are on the left, then a beaver dam and dens on the right.
- Cross the seventh wooden bridge. Enjoy wetlands on both sides of the path.
- Continue on a long stretch through a wooded area.
- The land again turns to wetlands, this time with clumps of wild daylilies along the shore.
- The path ends at the yellow gates at Cayward Cross Road. From here you have two options. One is to turn around and follow the rail trail back to the start. The other is to follow the roads back. The roads have good paved shoulders and are predominately downhill. Turn right (E) onto Cayward Cross Road, right onto Route 245, then right again when it ends at Route 21. This takes you back to the start. Along the way, pass an old cemetery and a roadside farm stand.

Date Enjoyed: _____

Notes:

Rides Southwest of Rochester

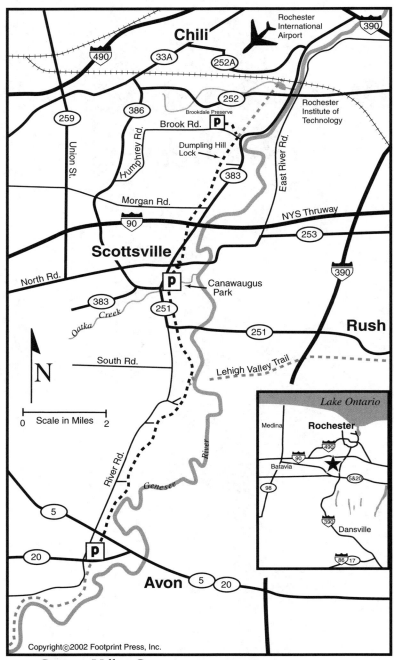

Rochester International Airport

Chili

490

33A

252A

252

386

Brookdale Preserve

Brook Rd.

P

Rochester Institute of Technology

259

Humphrey Rd.

Dumpling Hill Lock

East River Rd.

383

Morgan Rd.

90

NYS Thruway

Scottsville

253

North Rd.

P

Canawaugus Park

390

383

251

Oatka Creek

251

Rush

South Rd.

Lehigh Valley Trail

N

0   Scale in Miles   2

Lake Ontario

Medina   **Rochester**

490

90

Batavia

5&20

98

Genesee River

River Rd.

390   Dansville

5

86   17

20

Avon   5   20

Copyright©2002 Footprint Press, Inc.

Genesee Valley Greenway - Chili to Avon (north section)

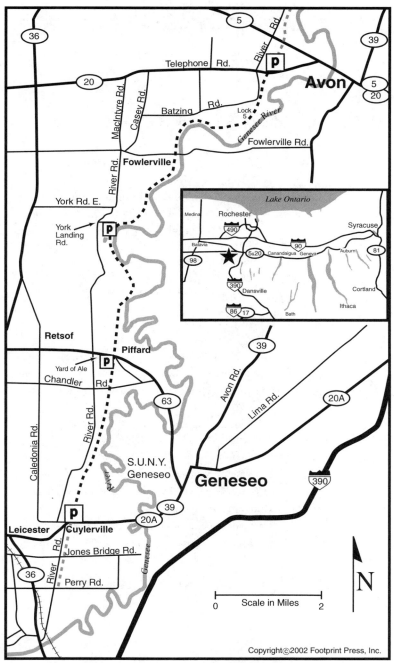

Genesee Valley Greenway - Avon to Cuylerville (south section)

35.

Genesee Valley Greenway (Chili to Cuylerville)

Location:	West of the Genesee River, from Chili, to Cuylerville, Monroe & Livingston Counties
Parking:	From Rochester, head south on Scottsville Road (Route 383). South of Route 252, turn west onto Brook Road. The parking area will be on your right, next to yellow metal gates. There is room for 4 cars.
Alternative Parking:	A short trail from the Brook Road parking area leads to Brookdale Preserve which has a large parking lot.
	Canawaugus Park parking lot (south of the village of Scottsville, off Route 251)
	Route 20 (Telephone Road), at the trail crossing, 0.9 mile west of the Route 5 junction
	At the end of York Landing Road, off River Road (a large parking lot)
	Route 63, at Yard of Ale Canal House Inn (3226 Genesee Street, near Flats Road)
	The bend in Route 20A in Cuylerville
Riding Time:	4 hours one way
Length:	25.6 miles one way (smaller segments are possible)
Difficulty:	Moderate, some mild hills
Surface:	Crushed stone, mowed grass, packed dirt
Trail Markings:	White metal "Genesee Valley Greenway" signs and yellow metal gates at road crossings
Uses:	

Facilities: Restaurants near the trail in Scottsville and Piffard,
              picnic tables in Canawaugus Park
Dogs: OK on leash
Admission: Free
Contact: Friends of the Genesee Valley Greenway, Inc.
              PO Box 42, Mount Morris, NY 14510
              (585) 658-2569
              www.fogvg.org

              NYS DEC, Regional Land Manager
              7291 Coon Road, Bath, NY 14810
              (607) 776-2165
              www.dec.state.ny.us

The Genesee Valley Greenway will eventually stretch 90 miles. It's an historic and natural-resource corridor that follows a transportation route used by the Genesee Valley Canal, from 1840 to 1878, and later by the railroad, from 1880 to the mid-1960s. The former rail bed now serves as a multi-use greenway trail open to hikers, bikers, horseback riders, cross-country skiers, and snowmobilers. Currently 54 miles of the total 90 miles are open for use. Each year more segments are opened. The trail connects with the Rochester River Trail, the Erie Canalway Trail, the Finger Lakes Trail, as well as Rochester's Genesee Valley Park and Letchworth State Park. Eventually it will connect to the Mendon Lehigh Trail via a bridge over the Genesee River.

The Genesee Valley Greenway passes through wetlands, woodlands, rolling farm lands, steep gorges, historic villages, and the Genesee and Black River valleys. It offers something for everyone from a short ride to a challenging long-distance trek. You can stop to explore quaint villages, visit an historic canal-era inn, or inspect well-preserved stone locks and other remnants of the ingenuity and engineering that built the canal and the railroad.

Forget your preconception of a converted railroad trail. On this trail you're in for some pleasant surprises. Rather than proceeding straight as an arrow, the trail meanders to follow the sweeping curves of the Genesee

River. And, it's not particularly flat. Not that it's hilly, but it does have lots of little hills and dales, which make the ride interesting. The bed is well-packed, so that this off-road trail is fairly easy to pedal.

Swinging in for a dip in Oatka Creek near George Bridge in Scottsville.

It's hard to match the views along here in the spring, summer and fall. But give it a try when the trees are bare in order to get the full view of the winding Genesee River and the dramatic eroded gorges as water rushes to the river.

The Genesee River begins its northward journey as a small stream in a farmer's field in Pennsylvania and flows 147 miles to Lake Ontario. Native Americans fished the river's waters and traveled its length by canoe. Early settlers used its power to grind grain into flour and to saw trees into lumber. Later, industrial mills harnessed the power to forge iron into parts and weave cotton into cloth. Today the river is a source of recreation and beauty, and its power is still used to generate electricity. The dam at Mount Morris manages the flow of this important waterway.

This country ramble takes you past fields of many varieties, lots of farm lanes, and plenty of wild animals. We got spectacular, close-up looks at a coyote, fox and a turtle, as well as the more mundane squirrels, cows, horses, geese, deer, and even a cat.

The Genesee Valley Canal was built between 1836 and 1862 to connect Rochester to the Allegheny River. It was never an economic success. It closed in 1878, suffering from competition by railroads, lack of water during droughts, and high maintenance costs. The land was sold to the Pennsylvania Railroad in 1880 and operated from 1881 to 1963, between Rochester and Olean. Mud slides in Letchworth Gorge among other problems led to the railroad's demise.

The first canal artifact you'll pass will be Lock 2, the Dumpling Hill Lock, one of the best preserved locks on the Genesee Valley Canal that operated from 1840 to 1878. The canal's original 115 locks were made of either wood, a combination of wood and stone, or all stone. Over the years the wood rotted and most locks deteriorated or were lost altogether. But this 90-foot-long, 15-foot-wide lock is all stone and well preserved. Each lock had a lock keeper and sometimes a lock house. The Dumpling Hill Lock had a house which was located west of the canal near Coates Road.

Canawaugus is Seneca Indian for "The Place of Stinking Water" because of the nearby sulphur springs. From the parking area at Canawaugus Park, look across to the north side of Oatka Creek to see an old feeder gate for the Genesee Valley Canal. A feeder gate consisted of a lock, dam, and toll house.

Next comes remains of the cut-stone Lock 5 and several ponds that originally served as turning basins for the Genesee Valley Canal.

As you bike along, note the presence of stately old oak trees standing in the middle of a number of farm fields. Years ago, red oak and shagbark hickory were the dominant trees in the forests of upstate New York. But, by the early 1900s the forest cover was down to ten percent of its original level, as farmers cleared land for fields and harvested the lucrative lumber. A few oaks were spared. Their broad canopy provided shade for

207

farmers and their animals as they toiled in the fields. Some of these oaks are over 200 years old.

This public trail is ours to enjoy thanks to the Friends of the Genesee Valley Greenway, the Department of Environmental Conservation, and New York State Office of Parks, Recreation, and Historic Preservation (OPRHP).

Distance Between Parking Areas:

Brook Road to Canawaugus Park	4.6 miles
Canawaugus Park to Route 20	8.4 miles
Route 20 to York Landing Road	5.9 miles
York Landing Road to Route 63	2.9 miles
Route 63 to Route 20A	3.8 miles

Trail Directions

- Begin by heading south on the trail from the parking area. (A short trail off this parking area leads to Brookdale Preserve with a big parking lot.) (The trail goes north from here but it dead ends at active railroad tracks. With a ride along busy Route 383 you can connect to the remainder of the Genesee Valley Greenway into Genesee Valley Park. See Trail #6 on page 54.)
- Pass Dumpling Hill Lock on your right at 0.8 mile.
- Cross two farm lanes. The ditch to your right was once the Genesee Valley Canal.
- Cross Morgan Road.
- Cross a gravel driveway.
- Pass under the New York State Thruway.
- The path narrows and heads uphill to Route 383. Follow the path right to parallel Route 383 to a small graveyard with the gravestone of Joseph Morgan, a Revolutionary War captain. He is credited with being the first settler in Chili in 1792.
- Cross Route 383 with care, being certain that you can see oncoming traffic far enough ahead for a safe crossing. Look for the trail on the left at the end of the guard rail and head downhill.
- Bear right at the base of the hill to return to the wide Genesee Valley Greenway Trail.

- Pass Rodney Farms, a thoroughbred horse farm, on the left.
- Cross Route 253 at 4.0 miles.
- Pass a house & farm lane.
- A boardwalk/bridge winds its way up to the village of Scottsville from the right. Scottsville has a variety of restaurants that offer food and ice cream.
- Cross Oatka Creek at 4.8 miles on the plate girder bridge (former Pennsylvania Railroad bridge) known locally as the "George Bridge." Notice the swing rope hanging over Oatka Creek from the north shore. Anyone for a dip?
- The trail is mowed grass for a short while through Canawaugus Park. Picnic tables are available here.
- Cross two driveways, then a tractor path.
- Cross Route 251. The old canal bed reappears to your right.
- Cross three tractor paths.
- At 7.0 miles, cross over a small creek on a bridge.
- Pass the Lehigh Railroad trestle, spanning a quarter mile over the Genesee River. This area was known as Wadsworth Junction. There's a small side loop on the river side. Some day this bridge will be redecked to connect to the Mendon - Lehigh Valley Trail.
- Pass two ponds on the right.
- Cross a farm path with a house to the right.
- Pass a beaver pond drainage running under the trail.
- At 9.0 miles, pass a large "Warning - No Trespassing" sign.
- Cross a road to a farm house.
- Pass underground gas pipeline #65.
- Cross a tractor path.
- Cross Route 5 at 12.4 miles.
- Cross Route 20 at 13.3 miles.
- Cross a tractor path. The trail in this section is a narrow double-track of cinder and dirt.
- The trail jogs to the right at a farm lane.
- Cross a gravel road.
- When you see two benches on the left, look right to see the remains of Lock 5, built about 1840.

- If the grass has recently been mowed, watch for segments of old rails still buried in the grass.
- The Genesee River appears on the left.
- Continue straight on a short stretch of gravel driveway.
- Cross Fowlerville Road. The trail widens and is fresh packed gravel.
- Ride a sunny stretch (no tree canopy). After crossing three tractor paths the trail reverts back to double-track.
- A culvert diverts water under the rail bed as creek water makes its way to the river.
- At 18.9 miles pass a pond and bench on the left, then the York Landing parking area. York Landing was the site of an early settlement. There was a turning basin in the canal to facilitate cargo loading from the mills. The ponds you see are remnants of the old turning basin.
- The trail will be stony for about 1/8 mile.
- Cross three tractor paths.
- Pass the fence of Atofina Chemicals, Inc..
- At 21.8 miles cross Route 63. Parking is available at the Yard Of Ale Restaurant which serves lunches and dinners daily.
- The trail is now four feet wide. Cross Chandler Road. (The area to your left was once a Tuscarora Indian village called O-HA-GI.)
- Cross a tractor path and pass farm ponds. Notice the view of SUNY Geneseo buildings on the hillside to the left.
- Pass a tractor path to the left.
- Cross a tractor path and continue straight as the trail narrows to rougher double-track.
- Cross a bridge with black metal rails over a creek feeding the Genesee River.
- Pass a series of large swamp ponds.
- Reach the parking area in Cuylerville. There is only room for a few cars. Do not block the trail. (The trail continues south to Perry Road but no parking is available there.)

Date Enjoyed: _____

Notes:

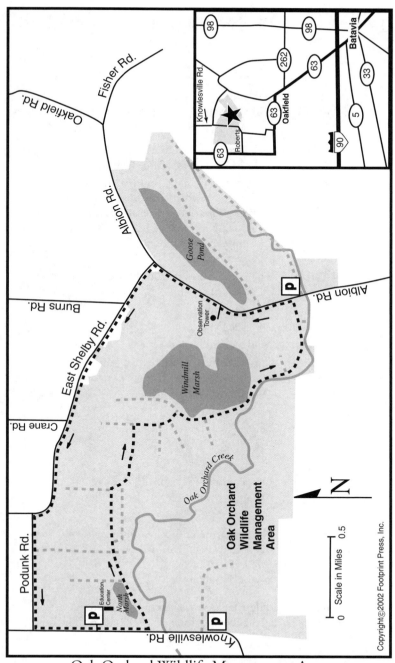

Oak Orchard Wildlife Management Area

36.
Oak Orchard Wildlife Management Area

Location:	Oak Orchard Wildlife Refuge, Alabama (northwest of Batavia), Genesee County
Parking:	From Batavia, follow Route 63 north. Turn east on Roberts Road and north on Knowlesville Road. The Education Center parking area, on the west side of Knowlesville Road, is marked with a large yellow & brown "Oak Orchard, State of NY, DEC" sign.
Alternative Parking:	The parking area on Albion Road, north of Oak Orchard Creek
Riding Time:	1.25-hour loop
Length:	7.8-mile loop
Difficulty:	Moderate, hills on the roads
	(Easy, 7.0 miles round trip, if you go out and return on the dikes rather than returning via roads.)
Surface:	Dirt, gravel, and packed-grass tire tracks left by State vehicles
Trail Markings:	None
Uses:	
Facilities:	Observation tower on Albion Road
Dogs:	OK on leash
Admission:	Free
Contact:	NY. Department of Environmental Conservation 6274 E. Avon-Lima Road, Avon, NY 14414 (585) 226-2466 www.dec.state.ny.us

Oak Orchard Wildlife Management Area is the easternmost of three adjacent wildlife areas that cover a total of 19,000 acres. The other two areas are Tonawanda Wildlife Management Area and Iroquois National Wildlife Refuge. Oak Orchard Wildlife Management Area is located in an historic wetland known as "The Oak Orchard Swamp," created by a natural barrier across Oak Orchard Creek. This barrier is an outcropping of limestone located at Shelby Center that resisted the cutting action of the creek and created a huge wetland upstream. Historically, spring flooding of Oak Orchard Creek provided temporary water areas for migrating waterfowl, but by late spring, water levels would drop, leaving only a scant nesting habitat.

After the State acquired the land, wetland habitats were restored through the construction of perimeter dikes to create large impoundments of marsh vegetation. To provide the best possible habitat for wildlife, water levels in the impoundments are manipulated to create conditions that provide a mix of underwater plants, emergent vegetation, and open water.

Natural, undisturbed marshes thrive because of fluctuating water levels, which result from precipitation or lack of it. Periodic drying is important for the longevity of a marsh. During dry times the marsh soil is exposed to air, which allows it to consolidate, thus providing a good foothold for new plants. Dead organic matter decomposes and replenishes nutrients for growing plants. The dried soil provides an excellent bed for seed germination. To simulate this natural process, the Department of Environmental Conservation (DEC) periodically drains areas of the marsh.

The primary objective for Oak Orchard Wildlife Management Area is to provide emergent marsh and grassland habitats for a variety of wildlife. Birding is best in the area from March through November, with peak waterfowl migrations occurring in mid-April and early October.

If you ride this area in summer, you'll notice a vivid carpet of purple flowers. Although pretty to look at, purple loosestrife is a detriment to the marshes. Purple loosestrife is not a native plant. In the 1800s seeds were brought to North America in the ballast holds of European ships. Since its introduction, it has spread rapidly across the continent. Once this plant gets a foothold, the habitat where fish and wildlife feed, seek

213

shelter, reproduce, and rear young quickly becomes choked under a sea of purple flowers. Public and private groups across the continent have banded together in unparalleled cooperation to manage the purple loosestrife problem through education and eradication efforts.

This is an active hunting ground so we don't recommend bicycling here in the fall. If you are bicycling during hunting season, be sure to wear plenty of blaze orange clothing.

The trails you'll ride are on the dikes around the marsh areas. The surface is dirt, gravel, and packed grass tire tracks from State vehicles. It's easy to follow—just stay on the most heavily warn track areas. You may want to choose an overcast or cool day for your ride because there is no tree cover. Take binoculars for spotting birds and other wildlife. We saw several deer along the way. Great blue herons took off in front of us, spreading their large wings and trailing their long legs. Once a safe distance away, they squawked their displeasure at us. We even saw an eagle take flight across the marsh.

You have two options for this ride. Head out and back on the dikes for a total of 7 easy miles or head out on the dikes and return on the more hilly paved roads for a 7.8-mile loop.

Trail Directions
- Turn left (S) out of the Education Center parking area onto Knowlesville Road.
- In 0.2 mile, turn left onto the trail, passing a yellow metal barricade.
- Pass a nest stand on the left. (Are any osprey in residence?) North Marsh Pond is also on your left. (As you ride, you'll pass a series of small ponds and flooded areas on both sides of the dike. Some of these are potholes, dug as watering holes for the deer and other wildlife.)
- Pass mowed-grass dikes on both sides. Stay on the gravel tracks.
- At the "T," turn right (S).
- At 1.4 miles the main trail bends left (SE) past a trail to the right.
- Pass a trail to the right. Water channels are now on both sides of the trail.
- Reach a "T" at 1.8 miles and turn right (S).

- Pass more mowed-grass dikes.
- At 2.3 miles, see the open water of Windmill Marsh Pond to the left.
- Pass a trail to the right and a water channel.
- Pass an old bridge across the channel to your right.
- The trail bends left over a culvert, with a small pond on the left.
- At 3.2 miles, the trail bends right (SE) through fields, with Oak Orchard Creek behind the trees to your right.
- Pass around a brown metal gate to Route 9 (Fisher Road). You've come 3.5 miles. (You can turn around and retrace your path to the parking area from here or take the more hilly paved road option for 4.2 miles back to the parking area.)

To return via road:
- Turn left (N) onto County Route 9 (Albion Road).
- Turn left (NW) on East Shelby Road.
- Continue straight past Burns Road.
- Pass a trail to the left.
- At 5.7 miles, cross a bridge.
- Continue straight past Crane Road.
- Pass a trail to the left.
- At 6.4 miles, the road bends right, then left. Stay on the paved road.
- Pass the Oak Orchard maintenance area.
- Reach the "T" of County Route 23 (Knowlesville Road) at 7.2 miles. Turn left (S).
- Only 0.5 mile left until the parking area at the Education Center.

Date Enjoyed: _____
Notes:

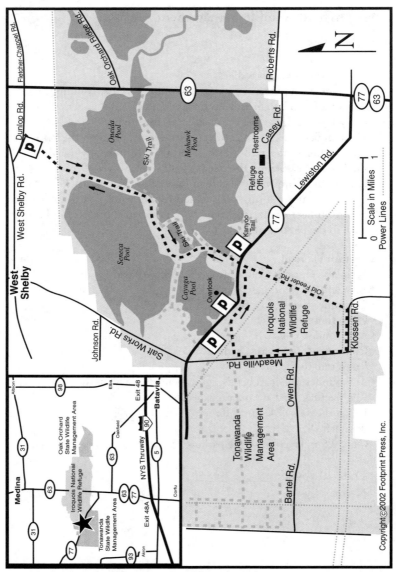

Iroquois National Wildlife Refuge and
Tonawanda Wildlife Management Area

37.
Iroquois National Wildlife Refuge and Tonawanda Wildlife Management Area

Location:	Iroquois National Wildlife Refuge and Tonawanda Wildlife Management Area, Alabama (north-west of Batavia), Genesee & Orleans Counties
Parking:	The parking area is on the north side of Route 77 (Lewiston Road) between Casey Road and Salt Works Road. It's marked with a large brown and white sign for "Kanyoo Trail" and has a big red barn at the back of the parking lot.
Alternative Parking:	The parking area on Dunlop Road, east of West Shelby Road
	Two other overlook parking areas along Route 77
Riding Time:	2-hour loop
Length:	12.5-mile loop
Difficulty:	Easy (more difficult if grass is unmowed or wet)
Surface:	Dirt, gravel, and packed grass tire tracks from State vehicles
Trail Markings:	None
Uses:	
Facilities:	Porta-Potty at the Kanyoo Trail parking area
Dogs:	OK on leash
Admission:	Free
Contact:	Iroquois National Wildlife Refuge 1101 Casey Road, Bascom, NY 14013 (585) 948-5445
	NYS Department of Environmental Conservation 6274 E. Avon-Lima Road, Avon, NY 14414 (585) 226-2466 www.dec.state.ny.us

Tire tracks form a hard-packed trail in Iroquois National Wildlife Refuge.

Iroquois National Wildlife Refuge and Tonawanda Wildlife Management Area join together with Oak Orchard Wildlife Management Area to form a total of 19,000 acres of impounded marshlands for the nurturing of wildlife.

Wildlife abounds on this trail, which in a previous era was called Feeder Road. On our trip, for example, deer watched from ahead on the path as we approached. Deciding we might be a threat, they leaped for cover with white tails flying. Great blue herons flew overhead, spreading large wings, and squawking their displeasure at us. White egrets spied us from treetops and fished in open pools.

This is an active hunting ground, so we don't recommend bicycling here in the fall. If you are bicycling during hunting season, be sure to wear plenty of blaze orange clothing.

Along the way you'll pass intersections with a ski trail several times. This is a 7.5-mile loop around Mohawk Pool that is open for cross-country skiing in the winter. The ski trail is managed for wildlife nesting during summer months and is not available for hiking or biking. Other trails, dikes, and service roads in the area are also off limits to bicycles.

The Kanyoo Trail is a 1-mile loop hiking trail that is described in the book *Take A Hike! Family Walks in the Finger Lakes & Genesee Valley Region*.

Trail Directions
- From Kanyoo Trail parking area turn right (NW) on Route 77 (Lewiston Road).
- Cross Lewiston Road and in 0.1 mile, turn left (SW) onto the gravel trail, after a guard rail. This is the south end of old Feeder Road.
- Ride straight past a brown metal gate. A canal is on the left.
- At 0.7 mile, pass under power lines and pass a trail to the left.
- Pass a trail to the right.
- At 1.3 miles, continue straight on the grass, past a trail to the left.
- Reach power lines and a gravel road at 1.6 miles. Turn right (W) on Klossen Road and ride between the two sets of power lines.
- The road reaches a "T" at 2.2 miles. Turn right (N) on pavement (onto Meadville Road).
- Pass houses.
- Pass Owen Road to the left.
- Pass a gravel trail to the right.
- Pass a path to the right with a barrier and stop sign.
- At 3.5 miles, immediately before a bridge over a canal with yellow and black striped signs, turn right (E) onto a dike and pass a barrier.
- At the top of the dike, turn left and follow the dike on packed grass.
- Pass under power lines at 3.9 miles.
- Pass a trail to the left. Continue as the trail bears right, parallel to Route 77.
- At 4.9 miles, reach a "T" and turn left (NE) on a gravel trail (old Feeder Road). Pass a metal barricade and cross Route 77. (You can return to the parking lot at this point if you prefer a shorter ride.)
- Pass another barricade across Route 77, then pass a trail to the left. The trail is now a wide gravel lane—what used to be Feeder Road.

- Pass a trail to the right with a yellow metal barrier. This is the ski trail.
- The gravel lane (Feeder Road) bends left. A dike heads off to the left, then the gravel lane bends right.
- At 5.6 miles, the ski trail heads off to the right. Stay on old Feeder Road.
- Enter a wooded area.
- At 5.9 miles, pass a service road into the woods on your left.
- Pass the ski trail to the right again at 6.3 miles.
- Enter a field area (riding east) with Oneida Pool to your right.
- Reach a junction with the ski trail to the right across the feeder canal. Continue straight (N) as the trail narrows.
- The feeder canal disappears into the woods to your right.
- Continue straight past a grass dike to the left.
- The trail bed turns to dirt as you enter the woods.
- Pass an old beaver dam in the feeder canal on the right.
- At 8.1 miles, pass overhead power lines and the buried gas line.
- At 8.7 miles, ride past the yellow metal barrier to the parking area on Dunlop Road.
- Turn around and retrace your path. (Or, return by roads, riding 5.5 miles rather than 3.8 trail miles. Turn left and follow Dunlop to West Shelby, then south, rather than taking busy Route 63.)
- At 11.5 miles, pass the service road to the right with a brown sign "Official Vehicles Only."
- Continue following the gravel path back to Route 77.
- Turn left to return to Kanyoo Trail parking area.

Date Enjoyed: _____

Notes:

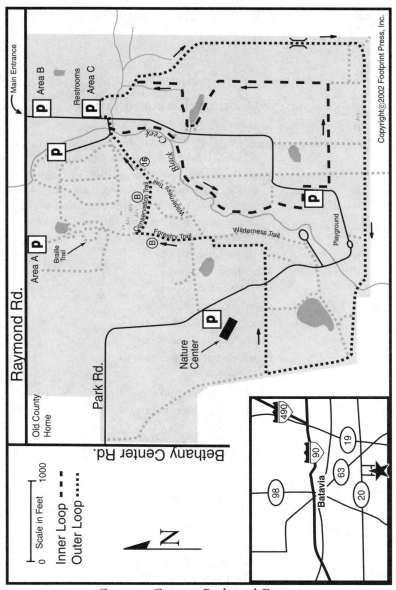

Genesee County Park and Forest

221

38.
Genesee County Park and Forest

Location:	Bethany (south of Batavia, bordering the Wyoming County boundary), Genesee County
Parking:	From Route 20, turn south on Bethany Center Road. Turn east on Raymond Road. Turn south off Raymond Road through the main park entrance onto Park Road. Park at the second parking area on the left (Area C).
Alternative Parking:	The first parking area (Area B)
Riding Time:	Inner loop: 25 minutes
	Outer loop: 45 minutes
	Combine both: 70 minutes
Length:	Inner loop: 1.6-mile loop
	Outer loop: 2.8-mile loop
	Combine both: 4.4-mile loop
Difficulty:	Difficult, hilly
Surface:	Hard-packed dirt and mowed-grass trails
Trail Markings:	Some junction number signs, some blazes and trail name signs

Uses:

Facilities:	Picnic pavilions, restrooms, fishing pond, playground, nature center with exhibits
Dogs:	OK on leash
Admission:	Free, 9 AM - 9 PM
Contact:	Genesee County Park and Forest
	11095 Bethany Center Road
	East Bethany, NY 14054
	(585) 344-1122

Genesee County Park and Forest is the first and oldest county forest in New York State and owes its existence to Genesee County opening a home for the poor and a residence for the care and confinement of lunatics.

The poor were orphans, habitual drunkards, and paupers, including any person who was blind, lame, old, decrepit, or vagrant. Lunatics were described as persons who had understanding but by disease, grief, or other accident, had lost the use of reason. This classification also included anyone of unsound mind caused by old age, sickness, or weakness who was unable to manage his own affairs. Oh, how things have changed! Some of the old buildings from the county home can still be seen on the corner of Bethany Center Road and Raymond Road.

In 1882, the county purchased a wood lot to supply the cooking and heating needs of the Poor House Farm and sold wood for $0.75 a cord to cover expenses. In 1915, about 31,000 trees were planted at a cost of $225. These trees were the beginning of the establishment of the forest. More evergreens were planted in the 1920s. 169,000 trees had been planted by 1935. The land was designated the first county forest in New York State.

Through the 1940s, 1950s, and 1960s, the county supervisors studied and discussed plans for a park. It wasn't until 1966 that funds were finally allocated. The Genesee County Park and Forest became a reality in 1971.

Today, this park is a gem rivaled by few others. Expanses of forest are interspersed with picnic areas, toboggan hills, horseshoe pits, volleyball courts, sandboxes, playgrounds, and baseball fields. Over the years, many volunteer groups have contributed to development of this park. In 1998, a group from Job Corps joined local volunteers to build a stunning nature center complete with stuffed animals and natural exhibits. Volunteers offer a variety of nature programs on subjects ranging from turtles, to blue birds, to backyard composting. The nature center is open from 3:30 PM to 9 PM on weekdays and 9 AM to 9 PM on weekends.

The park is open daily from 9 AM until 9 PM. There is a unique Braille and large print nature trail near Raymond Road in Area A. This walking-only trail is bordered by a coated link railing so the blind can walk along the trail and read the Braille interpretive signs. Unfortunately, as is true throughout the park, some of the signs have been disturbed by vandalism. The county continually works on replacing signs in the park.

Two loop trails are described below. You can ride them as separate adventures or combine them for a longer outing. The inner loop trail winds through hilly terrain in the woods. Sometimes you'll travel on narrow trails along Black Creek and sometimes on wide trails, but always shaded by a canopy of trees. Choose this route for a hot or sunny day. In addition to the hills, the challenge comes from riding over roots across the trail.

The outer loop trail is partially in the woods and partially through wide mowed swaths that can be warm when the sun is strong. It's challenging because of the hilly terrain and the mowed grass trails. This trail takes you into a less heavily used area of the park.

Inner Loop Trail Directions (designated by the long, dark dashed lines on the map)
- From the second parking area (Area C), head left (S) on Park Road.
- Take a quick right on the paved road.
- Immediately before the bridge, turn left onto the trail.
- Cross a cement bridge. This narrow gravel trail through the woods follows Black Creek.
- At the trail junction bear right and cross a boardwalk.
- Continue straight (SW) through a trail intersection. The terrain now gets hilly.
- Bear right at a "Y" junction and head uphill.
- At 0.7 mile, reach a parking area and turn left.
- Turn right onto Park Road.
- Take the first left (E), on a wide dirt trail, shaded by the woods. (A cable across the trail sports the sign "Official Vehicles Only.")
- Continue straight through two intersections.
- At 1 mile, reach a "T" and turn left (N).
- The terrain continues to be hilly.

- Turn right between the dike pond and the pavilion. (If you reach the road you rode too far.)
- Now a steep uphill to a "T." Turn right and continue uphill.
- The terrain will be hilly.
- Reach another "T." Turn left (NW).
  (To combine this loop with the outer loop, turn right at the "T.")
- Pass a pavilion and cross a creek to parking area C.

Date Enjoyed: _____

Notes:

Outer Loop Trail Directions (designated by the short, dark, dashed lines on the map)

- From the second parking area (Area C), head south past an "Authorized Vehicles Only" sign on the dirt trail.
- Cross two creeks.
- Bear left at the first junction and head uphill.
- Pass a trail to the right.
- At 0.8 mile, the trail turns right on a wide grass path. (A trail to the left is labeled "With Permission Only.")
- The trail will have a gradual downhill slope.
- Continue straight past two trails to the right.
- Continue straight through a trail intersection at 1.1 miles.
- At 1.2 miles, another trail will head off to the right. Continue straight, uphill.
- Cross two culverts, then pass a trail to the right.
- Climb a steep uphill grade. At the top of the hill, the main trail bends right and then heads down. Another trail on your right leads to a pond. The trees to your right are Norway spruce.
- At 1.7 miles, turn right and head downhill on another grass trail. To your left is a forest of white cedar.
- Cross a small wooden bridge.

225

- Pass a trail to the right and continue uphill.
- At 1.9 miles, cross Park Road. Continue uphill on the grass path.
- Pass a woods trail on the right.
- At 2.2 miles, reach the Wilderness Trail. Bear left on the Forestry Trail.
- Pass the second branch of the Wilderness Trail to the right. Stay on the Forestry Trail (green-blazed).
- Soon, reach another junction and continue straight on the Forestry Trail.
- The trail narrows, turns into dirt, and heads downhill through the woods.
- Turn right on the Conservation Trail (blue-blazed) before a small wooden bridge.
- Enter a pine forest. Continue straight past a trail to the right.
- At 2.6 miles, continue straight through junction #16.
- At 2.8 miles, turn right (E) on a road. Cross a bridge over Black Creek. (To combine with the inner loop trail, turn right on the dirt trail after the bridge.)
- Turn left at the stop sign onto Park Road.
- Parking area C is a quick right.

Date Enjoyed: _____

Notes:

226

Erie Canalway Trail

Erie Canalway Trail

Location:	Newark to Lockport, Wayne, Monroe, Orleans and Niagara Counties
Length:	94.5 miles
Difficulty:	Easy, mostly flat
Surface:	Paved (16.8 miles) and packed stone dust (77.7 miles)
Trail Markings:	Posts with round metal signs (brown, yellow, and blue) with a packet boat in the center and the words "Erie Canalway Trail" around the perimeter. No signs most of the way.
Dogs:	OK on leash
Contact:	New York State Canal Corporation 200 Southern Boulevard, PO Box 189 Albany, N.Y. 12201-0189 (800) 4CANAL4, www.canal.state.ny.us

Officially called the Erie Canalway Trail but more commonly known as the towpath, this trail stretches from Newark west to Lockport along the Erie Canal. It covers 94.5 miles and passes four working locks and 16 liftbridges along its route.

The 363-mile Erie Canal was opened with great ceremony in 1825. Dubbed variously "The Grand Canal," "Clinton's Folly," "Clinton's Ditch," and "The Big Ditch," the Erie Canal has been recognized as one of the great engineering feats of its day. With little technical knowledge or precedent to guide them, workers surveyed, blasted, and dug across New York State. They hewed through the hardest of solid rock, dug in infested marshes, devised and erected aqueducts to carry the canal across interrupting valleys and rivers, and constructed 83 locks to carry vessels through the variations in water height—one great set of locks rising nearly as high as the majestic falls of Niagara.

By connecting the Atlantic Ocean (via the Mohawk River) and the Great Lakes, the Erie Canal opened the West and initiated a great surge of commerce. Many communities that sprang up along the new canal

228

still carry their "port" names today, such as Lockport, Brockport, Spencerport, and Fairport. Those were the glorious days of life at a snail's pace as horses and mules towed boats along the canal at four miles per hour taking just under six days to make the trip from Albany to Buffalo. The packet boats, dandy drivers with stovepipe hats, mule teams, and "hoggee" mule drivers are long gone. Today the Erie Canal and its tow-path are used almost exclusively for recreation.

The canal was widened, deepened, and rerouted over the years to accommodate a succession of larger boats that hauled bigger loads. Initially the canal was kept separate from creek waters by use of aque-ducts and culverts. Later as engineering advanced, they learned how to control water levels in the canal and still merge it with natural waterways such as the Seneca and Genesee Rivers. In 1917 the enhanced canal was called the Barge Canal. Today we've reverted to the historic Erie Canal name.

The liftbridge in Medina is one of 16 liftbridges
along the Erie Canalway Trail.

Although the towpath is a long trail, you can ride it in segments because of the many access points. A truly enjoyable way to cover the entire length is by taking a several-day trip and staying overnight at the bed-and-breakfasts along the way. As a weekend getaway, park your car along the towpath, pedal out in a single direction, stay in a bed-and-breakfast overnight, and pedal back to your car the next day. The prevailing winds blow from the west, so for a two-way trip it's best to peddle west then return east when you're more tired. For a one-way trip you may want to consider reversing the directions and biking from west to east.

The towpath may be long, but it's one of the easiest trails to follow. When in doubt, choose a path close to the canal. You're likely to see boats — both recreational and tour boats regularly ply these waters during the summer months. It's fun to watch them pass under liftbridges and through the locks.

To present more manageable adventures, we've split the Erie Canalway Trail into the following segments, traveling east to west:

Newark to Palmyra (new, not mapped)
Palmyra to Pittsford (Trail #39)
Pittsford to Spencerport (Trail #40)
Spencerport to Albion (Trail #41)
Albion to Lockport (Trail #42)

Update: 2007 saw the opening of a new segment of Erie Canalway Trail. You can now begin (or end) 9.5 miles east of Palmyra in Newark. The current terminus of this ever-expanding trail is in a parking lot behind the Quality Inn on Route 88, north of the canal.

The new segment is picturesque and parallels the canal closely, thus is easy to follow. Near Newark there are rolling hills, and the wide water segment of the canal. Three new bridges carry you over Red Creek and Ganargua Creek, and you ride under the completed Aldrich Change Bridge (see page 233) before connecting to the older segment of the Erie Canalway Trail in Palmyra's Aqueduct Park.

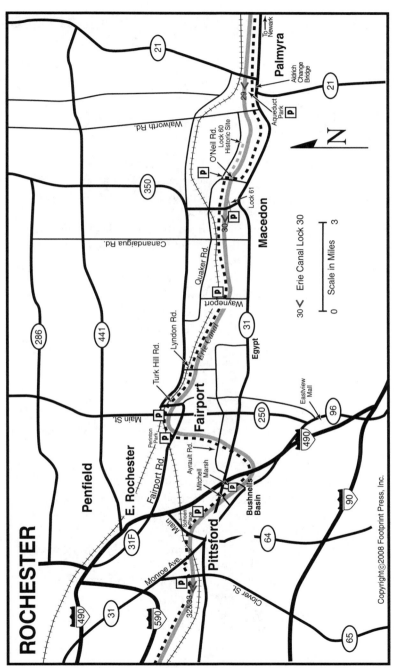

Erie Canalway Trail (Palmyra to Pittsford)

39.
Erie Canalway Trail (Newark to Pittsford)

Parking:	The parking lot behind Quality Inn on Route 88 (north side of canal), Newark
Alternative Parking:	Corner of West Shore Blvd. at Whitbeck/Stebbins Rd., Newark
	Aqueduct Park on the north side of Route 31, west of the village of Palmyra. Watch for the sign "Lock 29."
	O'Neil Road at the corner of Quaker Road
	Lock 30 on Route 350 in Macedon
	Wayneport Road, Macedon
	Box Factory lot on Lift Bridge Lane in Fairport
	Village lot behind Riki's Restaurant on Main Street, Fairport
	Perinton Park on Fairport Road, Fairport
	Behind Burgundy Basin Inn on Marsh Road, Fairport
	Village parking, next to the Coal Tower Restaurant, on Schoen Place, Pittsford
Riding Time:	4 hours one way
Length:	27.5 miles one way
Difficulty:	Easy, mostly flat (rolling hills at eastern end)
Surface:	Paved (3.5 miles through Fairport) and packed stone dust
Trail Markings:	Posts with round metal signs (brown, yellow, and blue) with a packet boat in the center and the words "Erie Canalway Trail" around the perimeter
Uses:	

Facilities: Many — see the description for each town
Dogs: OK on leash

Distances Between Parking Areas:

Rt. 88, Newark to Whitbeck Road	2.1 miles (not on map)
Whitbeck Rd. to Aqueduct Park, Palmyra	7.4 miles (not on map)
Aqueduct Park, Palmyra to O'Neil Road	2.1 miles
O'Neil Road to Lock 30, Macedon	1.0 mile
Lock 30, Macedon to Wayneport Road	3.3 miles
Wayneport Road to Main Street, Fairport	4.7 miles
Main Street, Fairport to Perinton Park	0.8 mile
Perinton Park to Marsh Road	3.3 miles
Marsh Road to Schoen Place	2.8 miles

Newark

The trail between Newark and Palmyra was built in 2007.

Palmyra

Settled in 1789 by John Swift, this area was originally called Swift's Landing. Joseph Smith founded the Mormon Church here in 1830. Visitors by the thousands now converge on Palmyra each July for the Mormon's Hill Cumorah Pageant, the largest outdoor religious extravaganza in the United States.

The current Erie Canal flows through Palmyra's historic Aqueduct Park, named for the remains of the Palmyra Aqueduct, built in 1857 on the original Erie Canal to carry water over Ganargua Creek (also called Mud Creek). The home of Lock 29, Aqueduct Park offers campsites, picnic tables, swing sets, a small boat launch, restrooms, and parking. The park is open from 9 AM to 9 PM. Lock 29 is one of 6 locks in Wayne County, the most of any county in the state.

Also in Aqueduct Park, is the 144-year-old Aldrich Change Bridge. A change bridge allowed mules towing barges and packet boats along the canal to reverse directions without having to be unharnessed and transported across the canal. The 74-foot-long, 14-foot-wide bridge was built

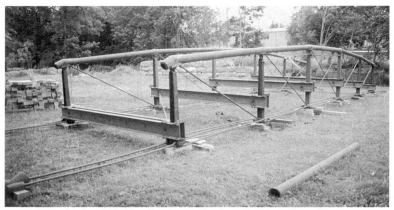

The Aldrich Change Bridge being reconstructed
to span the old Erie Canal bed.

by Squire Whipple in 1858. It was an ingenious piece of engineering, especially for the time. Originally it sat over the canal in Rochester. In 1880 it was relocated to the enlarged canal near the border between Macedon and Palmyra. It collapsed into Mud Creek in 1996 during an ice storm, but it was hauled out and restored by volunteers over a 6-year period. It is the oldest dated surviving composite cast iron bridge in NY State, and the only surviving canal change bridge. It now sits across the former canal bed which is the newest segment of Erie Canalway Trail.

B&B: Liberty House B&B, 131 W. Main Street, (315) 597-0011
        Canaltown B&B, 119 Canandaigua Street, (315) 597-5553

Trail Directions
• From the Quality Inn, Route 88, Newark, head west along the trail, north of the canal.
• Pass a pedestrian bridge over the canal to the left, then duck as you cross under Filkins/Stebbins/Whitbeck Road at 4 miles.
• Cross under Galloway Road. Pass Swift's Landing Park and ride over 3 bridges.

234

- Ride under Route 21, then reach Divison Street where you turn left to cross the bridge and continue west on the south side of the canal.
- Cross through Aqueduct Park, riding under the Aldrich Change Bridge.
- Ride over the Palmyra Aqueduct which was built in 1857.
- Head uphill to cross Walworth Road.
- At 11.6 miles, McDonald's and West Wayne Restaurant are across Route 31 to your left.

Macedon

On the way to Macedon you'll pass a side trail to Lock 60 Historic Site. Lock 60, a dual lock built in 1841 on the enlarged Erie Canal, was renovated by a volunteer group called the Lock 60 Locktenders. (See pages 92-95 for a description of the historic canal remnants and trails in the Macedon area.)

Macedon is home to the second working lock you'll encounter on this journey, Lock 30. At Lock 30 Canal Park on the south side of the canal, you'll find a campsite for hikers, bicyclists, and boaters with room for 4 tents, potable water, picnic tables, grills, and a restroom. The nearby railroad tracks are from the old New York Central Railroad. Just after Macedon, the canal widens in several places where the current canal was dug alongside the old one.

Trail Directions

- Head uphill as you approach O'Neil Road.
- Turn right and follow the sidewalk across the bridge, then take an immediate left to pick up the towpath. (The trail to Lock 60 is on your right.)
- Ride under pipes which carry materials from the Exon Plastics factory to railroad cars.
- Ride under Route 350 to Lock 30. There's parking on both sides of the canal at Lock 30.
- Cross Canandaigua Road. You've ridden 13.7 miles.
- The canal widens where the old and new canals merged.
- Cross Wayneport Road. There is a small parking lot here.

• At 18.1 miles ride under the Lyndon Road bridge. (A ramp was built to connect Lyndon Road and the Erie Canalway Trail in 2005.) Shortly, the path becomes paved.
• For a short section, the path is shared with cars.

Fairport

It's no exaggeration to say that Fairport owes its existence to the Erie Canal. Much of the area that is now Fairport was once a large swamp. Workers drained it while digging the canal, leaving fertile land instead of swampy ground. Farming prospered, and other businesses quickly sprouted along the canal to carry the harvest to Rochester and New York City. Fairport boasts the only slanted liftbridge along the Erie Canal. The bridge-tender's tower now houses modern computer equipment to control the bridge's movements. Fairport has restaurants, pizza, ice cream and coffee shops.

Bike Shop:	RV&E Bike & Skate, 40 N. Main Street, (585) 388-1350 (rentals available)
Ice Cream:	Lickety Splits Ice Cream Shop in the Box Factory building, 6 North Main Street, (585) 377-6250
Tours:	Colonial Belle Canal Tour and Dinner Boat, 400 Packett's Landing, (585) 223-9470
B&B:	Twenty Woodlawn B&B, 20 Woodlawn Avenue (585) 377-8224

Trail Directions

• At 19.6 miles a cement bridge abutment (from the Rochester, Syracuse & Eastern Railway) with colorful graffiti across the canal signals the terminus of the Perinton Hike-Bikeway Trail (Trail #18). There are plans to connect these two trails with a pedestrian bridge.
• Continue straight and ride under the Turk Hill Road bridge.
• Pass several gravel trails to the right that lead into Thomas Creek Wetlands with boardwalks and observation platforms overlooking the wetland. (See page 122 for a map.)
• Ride under Parker Street.

- On the right, just before the liftbridge is the Box Factory, which contains a restaurant, coffee shop and ice cream shop. Parking is available here. Fairport village also has several other restaurants, as well as donut, and pizza shops.
- Ride under the sloping liftbridge on Main Street. Walk your bike up a short flight of stairs.
- Ride through the edge of the village lot behind Riki's Restaurant on Main Street. Parking is available here.
- Pass Canalside Rentals (renting canoes, kayaks, and bikes, 585-377-5980).
- Pass the the old American Can Company building with its name spelled out in brick on the tall smokestack. It started life as the Sanitary Can Company in 1881.
- Ride through Perinton Park. It offers parking, picnic facilities, restrooms and swings facing the canal.
- Ride under Fairport Road (Route 31F).
- At 21.7 miles the pavement stops, and the trail reverts to packed stone dust.
- On the far side of the canal is a wide-water area, locally known as the oxbow, formed when the canal was enlarged, cutting off a loop from Clinton's Ditch. The island in front of the oxbow is the artificial result of many years of dredging.
- Ride under Ayrault Road.
- Ride under Pittsford-Palmyra Road (Route 31).
- At 24 miles pass guard gate #10.
- Ride under Interstate 490.

Bushnells Basin

In the early 1820s, before the Great Embankment was completed, Hartwell's Basin was the western terminus of the canal. After the full canal opened, William Bushnell operated a fleet of canal boats from the area, and the name was eventually changed to Bushnells Basin. In its heyday, the port at Bushnells Basin was a major shipper of agricultural products and a stop for the Rochester and Eastern Trolley line on its route between Rochester and Canandaigua. Richardson's Canal Inn (now an exclusive restaurant) started life as a hotel on the canal and trolley line.

The 70-foot-high Great Embankment was built to span the Irondequoit Valley. Irondequoit Creek now runs through a tunnel under the canal. Two metal guard gates stand at either end of the embankment. (For more detail see pages 135-136.)

Ice Cream: Abbott's Frozen Custard, 624 Pittsford-Victor Road, Bushnells Basin (585) 385-1366

B&B: Oliver Loud's Country Inn, 1474 Marsh Road, Pittsford, (585) 248-5200)

Trail Directions
•Traverse the Great Embankment with its cement walls rising 70 feet above the Irondequoit Valley below.
•Across the canal are Richardson's Canal House and Oliver Loud's Country Inn. They were a hotel, tavern, and stagecoach stop dating back to the early 1800s. Today they serve as a restaurant and bed and breakfast, respectively.
•Pass concrete abutments that used to carry the Rochester and Eastern Inter-Urban Trolley from Cayuga Lake to Canandaigua and Rochester.
•Ride under Marsh Road bridge at 24.6 miles. Across the Marsh Road bridge and to the right is Abbott's Frozen Custard and Pontillo's Pizza.
• Pass a trail to the right, leading to a parking lot behind Burgundy Basin Inn off Marsh Road.
• Pass Great Embankment Park with a dock, boat launch, and parking.

The tour boat *Sam Patch* stops at Pittsford to pick up passengers for Erie Canal cruises.

- Pass a guard gate at 26.3 miles.
- Ride under the Mitchell Road bridge.
- Ride under State Street (Route 31) bridge. The path again becomes paved. Across the canal is Oak Orchard Canoes (canoe rental, 585-682-4849).
- Schoen Place is on your right with restaurants, ice cream shops, and a bicycle shop. Village parking is available next to the Coal Tower Restaurant on Schoen Place. Please walk your bike through this congested section.

Pittsford

Pittsford was a thriving village well before the Erie Canal arrived. The big spring (water source) was used by the Iroquois Indians as a stopover point on their trade route through the area. The canal, even today, draws its water from the spring. Pittsford is home to Lock 32. Originally called Northfield, this town claimed Monroe County's first school, first library, first lawyer, and first physician. The name was changed to Pittsford in 1814.

A grain mill, which still operates on Schoen Place along the canal, attracted a wide variety of ducks. They have interbred to form some unusual combinations and now stay on the canal year round. It's tempting to feed the ducks, but please avoid the temptation. Feeding encourages large numbers of them to stay in close proximity. As a result of this unnatural congregation, a plague is spreading through their ranks.

Bike Shop:	Towpath Bike Shop, 3 Schoen Place, (585) 381-2808 (rentals available)
Ice Cream:	Bill Wahl's Ice Cream & Yogurt, 45 Schoen Place, (585) 248-2080
	Ben & Jerry's Pittsford Village, 5 S. Main Street, (585) 641-0735
Tours:	Sam Patch Tour Boat, 12 Cornhill Terrace (stops at Schoen Place), (585) 262-5661

Date Enjoyed: _____

Notes:

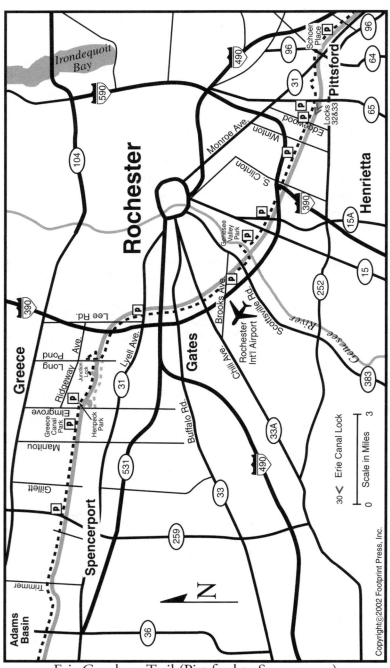

Erie Canalway Trail (Pittsford to Spencerport)

40.

Erie Canalway Trail (Pittsford to Spencerport)

Parking:	Village parking is available next to the Coal Tower Restaurant on Schoen Place, Pittsford
Alternative Parking:	Lock 32 Canal Park, Clover Street, Pittsford
	Lock 33 Canal Park, Edgewood Avenue, Henrietta
	South Clinton Avenue, Brighton
	Brighton Town Park, Westfall Road, Brighton
	Genesee Valley Park off Moore Drive, Rochester
	Holiday Inn, 911 Brooks Avenue, Rochester
	Lyell Avenue (Route 31), Rochester
	Henpeck Park, Greece
	Greece Canal Park, Greece
	Union Street (Route 259), Spencerport
Riding Time:	3.25 hours one way
Length:	19.1 miles one way
Difficulty:	Easy, mostly flat
Surface:	Paved (13.3 miles from Pittsford to Greece) and packed stone dust
Trail Markings:	None
Uses:	
Facilities:	Many — see the description for each town
Dogs:	OK on leash

Distance Between Parking Areas:

Schoen Place to Lock 32 Canal Park	1.7 miles
Lock 32 Canal Park to Lock 33 Canal Park	1.3 miles
Lock 33 Canal Park to South Clinton Avenue	1.7 miles
South Clinton Avenue to Brighton Town Park	0.6 mile

Brighton Town Park to Genesee Valley Park	2.1 miles
Genesee Valley Park to Holiday Inn	1.7 miles
Holiday Inn to Lyell Avenue	2.7 miles
Lyell Avenue to Henpeck Park, Greece	3.8 miles
Henpeck Park to Greece Canal Park	0.3 mile
Greece Canal Park to Union Street, Spencerport	3.2 miles

Rochester

The Erie Canal turned Rochesterville into a boomtown. Today it's the third largest city in New York State. The original Erie Canal traveled through the center of the city, across an 800-foot stone aqueduct. The second, sturdier version of the aqueduct was built in 1842 and is now the base of the Broad Street bridge. When the canal was widened and deepened into the Barge Canal, its route was redirected south of Rochester to its current location.

Locks 32 and 33 in this next section are the only locks on the system that are narrower at the bottom than at the top. No one really knows why they were built this way. However, as a result, barges that were tied side by side in the canal were squeezed as they descended. The two locks are close together, and in the days of heavy traffic, Lock 32 pulled water from Lock 33. A reservoir was built beside the canal near Lock 32 to provide water.

You'll pass through Genesee Valley Park on your way through the outskirts of Rochester. The trail takes you past four arched bridges; the third one crosses the Genesee River, another very important waterway in western New York State. The Genesee River - Downtown Loop Trail (see Trail# 7) and the Genesee Valley Greenway (see Trail #6) meet the Erie Canalway Trail in Genesee Valley Park.

Ice Cream: Keith's Frozen Kustard, Brooks Avenue, Rochester

Trail Directions
• From Schoen Place, head west on the towpath along the canal.
• Ride under the Main Street (Pittsford) bridge.

- Ride under an active railroad bridge.
- Ride under the Monroe Avenue (Route 31) bridge.
- Weekends and evenings you can continue straight along the canal. (This new segment was built in 2007.) At other times, you must follow the bypass route. Turn right at the NYS Canal Maintenance property onto Monroe Avenue, then turn left and follow the multi-use sidewalk on the south side of Brook Road. Bear left and return uphill to the towpath along the canal.
- 1.4 miles from Schoen Place, pass the Historic Erie Canal and Railroad Loop Trail heading off to your right (see Trail #20).
- Ride under the Clover Street (Route 65) bridge and uphill to Lock 32 and the Lock 32 Canal Park. Parking is available here.
- Cross a causeway over the mouth of the reservoir.
- At 2.8 miles pass the Jewish Community Center on your right.
- Ride under Edgewood Avenue.
- Carry your bike up some stairs to Henrietta Lock 33. This is the last lock for 65 miles until Lockport.
- Ride under Winton Road.
- Ride under South Clinton Avenue. You've come 4.7 miles.
- Ride under the twin bridges of Interstate 390 twice.
- Pass Brighton Town Park (entrance off Westfall Road) with parking.
- Ride under East Henrietta Road (Route 15A).
- Ride under West Henrietta Road (Route 15).
- Ride under Kendrick Road. You've come 6.6 miles.
- Pass two guard gates. These, and the set west of the Genesee River, protect the canal against any severe water level changes in the river.
- Pass two sets of abandoned railroad tracks (see Trail #28).
- Head downhill under Moore Drive in Genesee Valley Park.
- Pass two of the three gray, stone, arched bridges designed by Frederick Law Olmsted on your left. Red Creek enters the canal between these two bridges on the far side of the canal. Parking is available in Genesee Valley Park (off Moore Drive).
- Cross the Genesee River on the Waldo J. Nielson bridge. It's the third arched bridge you come to—the one with metal railings.
- Turn left immediately after the bridge. (To the right is the Genesee River - Downtown Loop Trail, Trail #7.)

A tug pushes a barge loaded with trees retrieved from the Genesee River, at the crossroads where the Genesee River and Erie Canal meet.

- Ride over the arched bridge over the canal (the third bridge built by Olmsted).
- Turn right before reaching the Interstate 390 bridge.
- Ride under Scottsville Road (Route 383). You've come 7.7 miles. The Greater Rochester International Airport will be to your left.
- Pass two guard gates.
- Pass an old abandoned railroad bridge.
- Pass the Holiday Inn on Brooks Avenue. Parking is available here.
- Ride across Brooks Avenue (Route 204). (Keith's Frozen Kustard is 0.4 mile west on Brooks Ave., opposite the airport.) You've come 8.6 miles.
- Cross the Rochester & Southern Railroad.
- Cross Chili Avenue (Route 33A). For the next 0.8 mile, the trail is double wide.
- At 10.1 miles, cross the bridge, high over the Conrail Railroad.
- Cross Buffalo Road (Route 33).
- Ride under Interstate 490 twice.
- At 11.3 miles cross Lyell Avenue (Route 31). Parking is available here.
- Ride under Lee Road.

Greece

The port of South Greece was a bustling canal town in the 1800s. It had a grocery store, apple dryhouse, post office, school, 25 houses and two doctor's offices, all now long gone, but replaced by a town with a population of approximately 90,000 people.

Trail Directions

- Ride under Interstate 390.
- Reach the Long Pond Road bridge at 13.3 miles. Turn left and follow the paved path to Long Pond Road.

    CAUTION: If you proceed straight and ride under the Long Pond Road bridge you'll have a short road ride on Elmgrove Road. (The path turns to stone dust. Enter Allen's Canalside Marina. Follow the driveway out to Elmgrove Road. After the bridge over the canal, turn right on Ridgeway Avenue and turn right into Henpeck Park. Bear right under the Elmgrove Road bridge and continue along the north side of the canal.)
- Turn right and ride the sidewalk across the bridge over the canal. (Ignore the Canalway Trail signs.)
- Turn right onto a paved bike path marked by a brown and white canal packet boat sign (just before Canal Landing Boulevard, the entrance road to an office park).
- At the canal, turn right and ride under the Long Pond Road bridge.
- The path turns to stone dust.
- At 13.8 miles pass Junction Lock with a simulated lock gate and 26-foot long beams to your right. This marks the route where the original canal looped north through Rochester. From here west, the current canal follows the original route of Clinton's Ditch.
- Ride through Henpeck Park. A short segment of trail is paved here. Henpeck Park offers picnic tables, grills, parking, and a Porta-Potty.
- Ride under the Elmgrove Road bridge.
- Pass Greece Canal Park at 15.8 miles. The entrance to Greece Canal Park is off Elmgrove Road. It offers parking, restrooms, picnic pavilions, a dock, a playground, sports fields and hiking trails (see *Take A Hike - Family Walks in the Rochester Area*).

245

- Ride under Manitou Road (Route 261).
- Ride under Gillette Road at 17.6 miles.
- Pass guard gate 11.
- Ride parallel to Canal Street.
- This section ends at Union Street (Route 259), Spencerport at 19.1 miles.

Date Enjoyed: _____

Notes:

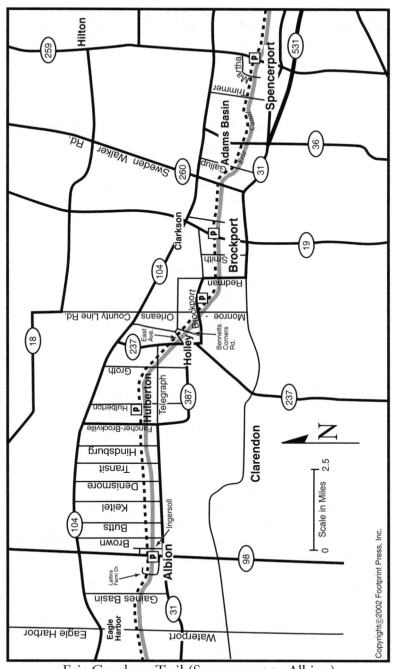

Erie Canalway Trail (Spencerport to Albion)

41.

Erie Canalway Trail (Spencerport to Albion)

Parking:	In Spencerport, park on the north side of the canal or along Union Street (Route 259)
Alternative Parking:	Main Street, Brockport
	Brockport Road (Route 31)
	Holley Park on East Avenue, Holley
	Hulberton Road
	Main Street, Albion
Riding Time:	4 hours one way
Length:	22.2 miles one way
Difficulty:	Easy, mostly flat
Surface:	Packed stone dust (some sections are slated to be paved in 2003)
Trail Markings:	None
Uses:	
Facilities:	Many — see the description for each town
Dogs:	OK on leash

Distance Between Parking Areas:

Union Street, Spencerport, to Main Street, Brockport	7.6 miles
Main Street, Brockport to Brockport Road (Route 31)	3.2 miles
Brockport Road (Route 31) to Holley Park	1.6 miles
Holley Park to Hulberton Road	3.1 miles
Hulberton Road to Main Street, Albion	6.6 miles

Spencerport

The settlement that began as Ogden Center in 1802 became Spencerport in 1825 after the canal was dug through Daniel Spencer's land. The original liftbridge control tower was moved to Pulver House Museum (696 Colby Street) in 1973. Today this bustling canal town offers several shops and restaurants including a pizza shop and coffee shop.

Bike Shop:	Sugars Bike Shop, 2139 North Union Street, (0.3 mile north of canal) (585) 352-8300 (rentals available)
Ice Cream:	Abbott's Frozen Custard, south of canal, 138 South Union Street
	Suey's Restaurant and ice cream, south of canal on Union Street

Trail Directions

- Cross Union Street (Route 259). A variety of restaurants are located along Union Street south of the bridge. Parking is available on the north side of the canal.
- Ride under the Martha Street bridge. There's a small parking area is available on Canal Street.
- Ride under the Trimmer Road bridge at 1.2 miles.

Adams Basin Bed and Breakfast was once a tavern.

• Eventually, the canal widens to a basin on the far side.

Adams Basin

Adams Basin was settled by William Adams and his family from Massachusetts in 1825, after the canal had opened. He built a business around a basin, dry-dock, and warehouse. The Adam's Basin B&B sits on the edge of the canal. It is reputedly the oldest tavern west of Rochester. The original bar is still in the house and dates back to 1827.

Notice the spillways, pumps and pipes erected along the canal as you bicycle. Farmers pay for the right to pump water from the canal to irrigate their fields.

B&B: Adam's Basin B&B, 425 Washington Street, (888) 352-3999

Trail Directions

• Cross Washington Street (Route 36) at 2.9 miles. The liftbridge is on your left and the Adam's Basin B&B on your right.
• Notice a waste weir across the canal.
• Parallel a road for 0.2 mile, then bear left to regain trail before Gallup Road.
• Ride under Gallup Road.
• Pass a boat launch across the canal.
• Ride under Sweden Walker Road (Route 260). You've come 5.4 miles.

Brockport

Brockport, which is located 40 miles west of Palmyra and 45 miles east of Lockport, is the halfway point for the Erie Canalway Trail. Now home to Brockport State University, this town gained fame in 1875 for the Globe Iron Works, which manufactured the first 100 McCormick reapers. The site of the old factory is now McCormick Park on the canal, near the Park Street bridge. Brockport is a village of Victorian architecture. The red brick houses in the town can be traced back to a once active brickyard and give rise to the nickname "Red Village." There are lots of restaurants, cafes, coffee and pizza shops in town, south of the canal and a few north of the canal.

Brockport boasts two liftbridges situated just 900 feet apart and operated by one person who dashes from one to the other.

Bike Shop: Bicycle Outfitters, 72 Main Street, (585) 637-9901

B&B: Victorian B&B, 320 Main Street, (585) 637-7519
              Portico B&B, 3741 Lake Road North, (585) 637-0220

Trail Directions
- Cross Fayette Street/Park Avenue next to the liftbridge at 7.6 miles.
- The pathway becomes simulated red brick and is lined with benches and lightposts.
- Cross Main Street (Route 19) past the liftbridge. Parking and picnic tables are available here. You'll also find Canalside Rentals (585-377-5980) where you can rent kayaks and bikes.
- The trail returns to stone dust.
- Ride under the Smith Street bridge. You've come 8 miles so far.
- Cross a metal grate over a spillway.
- Pass a small playground.
- Pass a guard gate.
- Ride under the Redman Road (Route 31) bridge at 9.2 miles.
- The trail becomes dirt and stone dust double-track but continues to be hard-packed and easy to ride.
- Pass a wide-waters area.
- Ride under the Brockport Road bridge (Route 31). Parking, a boat launch, a picnic pavilion and a Porta-Potty are available here, off Monroe-Orleans County Line Road.
- Ride under Bennetts Corners Road.
- Pass a waste weir across the canal. It forms Holley Canal Falls, a 35-foot high waterfall described in *200 Waterfalls in Central and Western New York - A Finders' Guide*.

Holley

Although he had no connection with the area, the village is named after Myron Holley. Mr. Holley was a member of the Canal Commission responsible for building the original Erie Canal. He is buried at Mount Hope Cemetery in Rochester. Holley has a beautiful canalside park with a gazebo, restrooms, showers, and a short hiking trail that leads to a pretty waterfall and the Historical Railroad Museum. The museum is housed in a restored railroad depot, circa 1907.

The Village of Holley operates a tent campsite near the canal for hikers, bicyclists, and boaters, with potable water, picnic tables, grills, and a restroom. South of the canal there are a diner & pizza shops in Holley.

As you bicycle west, notice the small blue "adopt-a-trail" signs along the path. Similar to the highway's adopt-a-road program, the NYS Canal Corp. encourages people to adopt a section of the Erie Canalway Trail and assist in its maintenance. New York Parks and Conservation Association manages this program. To learn more about the program and to receive an application package, please send an e-mail to canaltrail@nypca.org or call (581) 434-1583. Please include your name, address, group name (if any), day and evening telephone numbers, e-mail address and note the canal community you would like to work in.

B&B: Rosewood B&B, 68 Geddes Street, (585) 638-6186

Trail Directions
• Cross East Avenue, past the liftbridge labeled "Holley." Across the canal is a park with parking, rest rooms, a gazebo, and a trail to Holley Canal Falls. A left here is the shortest distance into the village of Holley.
• Ride under the Main Street (Byron-Holley Road) bridge (unlabeled) and pass a guard gate.
• Pass a wide-water area.
• Ride under the Telegraph Road bridge (unlabeled).
• Ride under the Groth Road bridge (unlabeled).
• Pedal over a short grass area then cross Hulberton Road past a lift-bridge. Past the bridge is a 2-car parking area, picnic tables, and a Porta-Potty.
• Repairs were made in 2002 to this section of the canal bank to stop leaks. Notice that the canal banks are now lined with pink colored stone. This is Medina sandstone, quarried from the numerous quarries dotting the area. Many local buildings are constructed using Medina sandstone.

- Ride under Fancher-Brockville Road. (Notice the many creeks flowing under the canal throughout this section. It's evidence that the canal is still in it's original position—dating back to a time when canal and creek waters had to be kept separate in order to control water level in the canal.)
- Ride under Hindsburg Road.
- Ride under Transit Road.
- Ride under Denismore Road.
- Ride under Keitel Road.
- Ride under Butts Road.
- Ride under Brown Street.
- Cross Ingersoll Street, passing a liftbridge.
- Cross Main Street, Albion, passing a liftbridge. Parking is available on both sides of the canal, near the Main Street bridge. Cross the bridge to find restaurants, a coffee shop and pizza shops.

Date Enjoyed: _____

Notes:

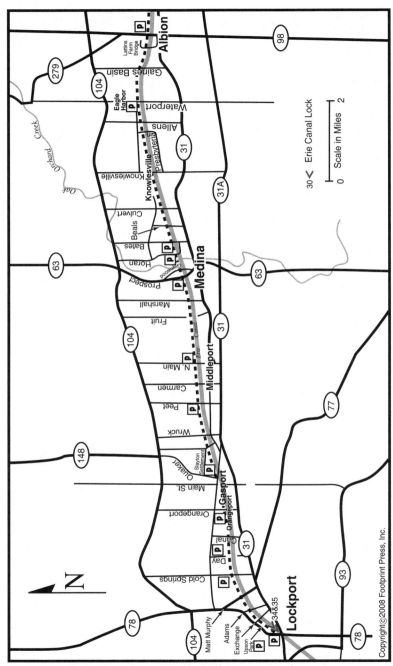

Erie Canalway Trail (Albion to Lockport)

N

Albion

98

279

104

Gaines Basin

Lattins Farm Bridge

Eagle Harbor

Waterport

Allens

31

Presbyterla

Knowlesville

31A

Culvert

Beals

Bates

Horan

Medina

63

Glenwood

63

Prospect

Marshall

Fruit

104

31

N. Main

Middleport

Erie Canal

Carmen

Peet

Wruck

148

Quaker

Slayton Settlement

Main St.

Gasport

Orangeport

Orangeport

Canal

31

Day

Cold Springs

Lockport

93

78

34&35

104

Matt Murphy

Adams

Exchange

Upson Park

78

77

Oak Orchard Creek

30 ◄ Erie Canal Lock

Scale in Miles
0   2

42.

Erie Canalway Trail (Albion to Lockport)

Parking:	Route 98, Albion, on both sides of the canal, near the Main Street bridge.
Alternative Parking:	Eagle Harbor
	Bates Road
	Horan Road
	Route 63, Medina, on the southern side of the canal
	North Main Street, Middleport
	Peet Street
	Bolton Street off Slayton Settlement Road
	Orangeport Road
	Day Road
	Cold Springs Road
	Upson Park in Lockport
	Downtown Lockport, along streets near the canal
Riding Time:	4 hours one way
Length:	28 miles one way
Difficulty:	Easy, mostly flat
Surface:	Packed stone dust, some mowed grass
Trail Markings:	None
Uses:	
Facilities:	Many—see the description for each town
Dogs:	OK on leash

Distance Between Parking Areas:

Route 98, Albion to Eagle Harbor	3.3 miles
Eagle Harbor to Bates Road	6.2 miles

Bates Road to Horan Road	0.8 mile
Horan Road to Route 63, Medina	0.6 mile
Rt. 63, Medina to N. Main St., Middleport	4.8 miles
N. Main St., Middleport to Peet Street	1.6 miles
Peet Street to Bolton Street, Gasport	2.9 miles
Bolton Street, Gasport to Orangeport Road	2.1 miles
Orangeport Road to Day Road	2.8 miles
Day Road to Cold Springs Road	0.9 mile
Cold Springs Road to Upson Park, Lockport	1.3 miles
Upson Park, Lockport to downtown Lockport	0.7 mile

Albion

Albion is the county seat of Orleans County. The town boasts a Methodist Church dating to 1860, a Presbyterian Church with a spire 175-feet tall, and a Greek Revival courthouse built in 1857 and located 1/4 mile south of the trail on Main Street (Route 98). Albion was the home of George Pullman, inventor of the Pullman railroad car. Legend has it that he conceived the idea while watching passengers on packet boats along the Erie Canal.

Three miles north of Albion is the Cobblestone Museum, offering history and examples of cobblestone architecture. 90% of cobblestone buildings can be found in this region of the Erie Canal. Most were built between the construction of the Erie Canal and the Civil War. (For more details, pick up a copy of *Cobblestone Quest - Road Tours of New York's Historic Buildings*.)

B&B: Friendship Manor B&B, 349 South Main Street (585) 589-7973
        Orchard View B&B, 3027 Densmore Road (585) 589-7702

Trail Directions
• Cross Main Street, Albion (Route 98). Public parking is available near the canal on both sides of the Main Street liftbridge.
• Ride under the Lattins Farm Drive bridge (it's access to private homes via West State Street) and past a guard gate.
• Ride under the Gaines Basin Road bridge. You've ridden 1.8 miles.

- You're now at the northernmost point of the Erie Canal.
- Pass a waste weir.
- Cross Waterport Road at Eagle Harbor in 3.3 miles. You have to carry your bike down a few steps or, bear right and follow the road around the liftbridge tender's house. Picnic tables, a Porta-Potty and parking are available here, 200 feet down Eagle Harbor-Knowlesville Road.
- Ride under Allens Road bridge. You've come 4.1 miles.
- Ride under the Presbyterian Road bridge.
- Pass a wide-waters area on the opposite side of the canal.
- Cross Knowlesville Road, passing a liftbridge and picnic tables. This is the 6.4-mile mark. South of the canal are a small grocery, deli, and sweet shop.

Oak Orchard Creek flows under the canal and cascades down a waterfall alongside the Erie Canalway Trail.

Medina

Medina grew on fertile land with ideal weather conditions for growing fruit. A curve in the canal made it a natural harbor for hauling produce as well as Medina sandstone. Just east of Medina, off Route 31, Culvert Road passes under the canal. Featured in *Ripley's Believe It Or Not*, it's the only road that passes under the Erie Canal. Built in 1823, it's an interesting sight and worth the side trip to take a look.

Medina also is home to the Medina Railroad Center. This museum of railroad memorabilia is located in a restored 1905 wood-frame freight house at 530 West Avenue, (585) 798-6106.

B&B: Garden View B&B and Llama Farm, 11091 Center
            Street Extension, Medina, (585) 798-1087

Culvert Road is the only road to run under the Erie Canal.

Trail Directions
- At 8.0 miles watch for the cement walls in the canal where Culvert Road runs under the canal. It was built in 1823 and is the only road to run under the canal. A steep path to the right leads down to the culvert. Leave your bike and take a short hike down to walk in the tunnel and let Erie Canal waters drip on your head.

258

- Ride under Beals Road.
- Cross Bates Road. Follow the trail left around the bridge and a new guard gate. There's a large parking area here with a boat launch, picnic tables and grills.
- At 10.5 miles ride under the Horan Road bridge. There are parking areas on both sides of this bridge, north of the canal.
- Oak Orchard Creek runs under the canal. Look for the waterfall to the right as you cross the creek, then continue on a cement dike which separates the creek from the canal.
- Ride under Glenwood Avenue. (After the bridge, take the trail to the right and follow the sidewalk up and over the Glenwood Avenue bridge for the closest access to downtown Medina shops and restaurants.)
- Reach the Route 63 (Prospect Avenue) liftbridge at 11.2 miles. Parking, picnic tables and grills are available across the liftbridge.
- Garden View B&B is across the canal.
- Ride under Marshall Road.
- Pass a boat launch on the south side of the canal.
- Pass guard gate 16 at 14.4 miles.

Middleport

Middleport has a diner (that sells ice cream) and pizza/sub shop. Two bridges further west is Canal Country Inn, a bed and breakfast.

B&B: Canal Country Inn, 4021 Peet Street, (716) 735-7572

Trail Directions
- Cross North Main Street, passing a liftbridge at 16 miles. Parking is on the north side of the canal before the bridge. Picnic tables are after the bridge. Middleport is south of the canal.
- Ride under Carmen Road.
- Ride under the Peet Street bridge (closed to motorized traffic). Parking is available on the north side of the canal. Canal Country Inn is across the canal. You've ridden 17.5 miles.
- Pass a waste weir on the opposite side of the canal.

Gasport/Orangeport

Gasport has a restaurant and pizza shop south of the canal. You won't see a village as you pass through Orangeport. You're in remote country settings.

B&B: Country Cottage B&B, 7745 Rochester Road, Gasport, (716) 772-2251

Trail Directions
- Ride under the Wruck Road bridge (unlabeled).
- Ride under Slayton Settlement Road bridge.
- Pass a private playground to the right, modeled like an old pirate ship. Notice the goats in a pen nearby. Across the canal is a marina and boat launch.
- To your right will be a parking area (it's at the end of Bolton Street).
- Cross a metal grate bridge over a spillway at 20.5 miles.
- Pass a new guard gate.
- Pass the Main Street, Gasport liftbridge at 21.3 miles.
- Ride under Orangeport Road. Parking is available here, accessible from Berner Parkway.
- Ride under Canal Road.
- Ride under Day Road (closed to motorized vehicles). You've come 25.1 miles. Parking, picnic tables and grills are available here (with access off North Canal Road).
- Ride under Cold Springs Road. Parking is available. The Widewaters Marina and Canal Park are visible across the canal.

Lockport

The trail ends at a flight of two locks, Locks 34 and 35. This is where the canal climbs 50 feet up the Niagara Escarpment. To the left are the original "Famous Five" stair locks, now relegated to water overflow. On the original canal, these five paired locks allowed simultaneous travel in

Locks 34 and 35 are paired in Lockport to raise boats
up and down the Niagara Escarpment.

either direction. One flight was replaced by the modern two-step locks which operate today. At the base of the locks is the old hydraulic power house, which supplied electricity to operate the locks and liftbridges. Today it's the New York State Erie Canal Museum, a great place to learn more of the canal's history. There are lots of restaurants in downtown Lockport.

Tours: Lockport Locks and Canal Tours, P.O. Box 1197,
     14095, (716) 693-3260
     MidLakes Navigation Company, 3 day cruises from
     Lockport to Syracuse and packet boats for hire,
     (800) 545-4316
     Lockport Cave & Underground Boat Ride, boat rides
     through a man-made cave, (716) 438-0174

B&B: Hambleton House B&B, 130 Pine Street, (716) 439-9507

Trail Directions
• Ride under the Matt Murphy Way bridge. You're 1.3 miles from the end.

- Pass the Adams Street liftbridge.
- Pass the Exchange Street liftbridge. Only 0.7 mile to go.
- Turn right through a brown gate and follow the trail around a maintenance area. Notice the dry dock inside the fenced area.
- Pass the remains of a pulp mill and old power plant to the right in Upson Park. The 2,430 foot-long raceway tunnel was built in 1858. Access to Upson Park which has parking, picnic tables & grills, is off Route 78.
- Ride under the railroad bridge. Pavement begins. Notice the Erie Canal Museum ahead.
- Pass Locks 34 and 35 as the path takes you up the Niagara Escarpment and under a bridge. The path ends here. (Plans call for extending the trail from Lockport to Amherst, via Tonawanda in 2003.) Parking is available along the streets near the locks.

Date Enjoyed: _____

Notes:

Additional Resources:

Bike Clubs:

Genesee Valley Cycling Club
7 Woodruff Glen
Rochester, New York 14624
ride line: (585) 234-5034
http://gvcc.11net.com
A group devoted to road racing.

Greater Rochester Eating and Tandeming Society (GREATS)
www.frontiernet.net/~tbg/greats
Tandem bike riders group.

Huggers Ski Club - Pedal Power
P.O. Box 23921
Rochester, NY 14692
hotline (585) 865-7910
www.huggersskiclub.org
Recreational cycling, beginner to advanced.

Rochester Area Recumbent Enthusiasts (RARE)
http://home.rochester.rr.com/rare
Recumbent bike riders group.

Rochester Area Triathletes (RATS)
www.rochestertriathletes.com

Rochester Bicycling Club, Inc.
P.O. Box 10100
Rochester, NY 14610-0100
(585) 238- 3254
www.rochesterbicyclingclub.com/WordPress
Road and mountain biking groups.

Western New York Mountain Biking Association
P.O. Box 1691
Amherst, NY 14226-7691
www.wnymba.org

General Information:

BikeRochester.com
Information and links to all things bicycling related in the Genesee
Valley Region, the Finger Lakes Region, and Rochester.
www.bikeRochester.com

Other Local Bicycling Guidebooks:

Cyclotour Guide Books
PO Box 10585, Rochester, NY 14610
(585) 244-6157
email: cyclotour@cyclotour.com
www.cyclotour.com
Road cycling travel books & tour guide books covering the Erie Canal,
Lake Ontario, Lake Erie, Lake Michigan, Finger Lakes, Lake Huron,
and cycling destination guides for canaling & bicycling in France &
New Zealand.

Footprint Press, Inc.
303 Pine Glen Court, Englewood, FL 34223
email: info@footprintpress.com
www.footprintpress.com
Bicycle trail guidebooks for Central and Western New York.

Bicycles Built for Women:

Terry Precision Cycling
1657 East Park Road, Macedon, NY 14502
(800) 289-8379
www.terrybicycles.com

The Recycle Cycle Program

Clean out your garage, basement and storage rooms. Bring any used, working condition bikes to a local independent bicycle shop. Genesee Valley's independent bicycle dealers have arranged with the Salvation Army to collect used bicycles in working condition, rehabilitate them, and distribute them to disadvantaged adults and children in need of reliable transportation.

Neither the Salvation Army nor the bicycle shops will sell the donated bicycles. You will receive a Salvation Army donation form to declare a value for your charitable donation to reduce your tax liability.

To donate a bicycle, call your local bike shop and ask if they participate in the Recycle Cycle Program. Then, prepare your bicycle for donation. Recycle Cycle wants donated bicycles that are in usable condition. They recommend but do not require that you:

- Do a visual inspection of the bike.
- Use a garden hose to wash your bicycle.
- Spin the chain and pedals.
- Move the shift gears to see if they are working.
- Fill flat tires. (Look on the tire to find how much pressure is needed.)

Then deliver the bicycle to your local independent bicycle shop. The bicycle shop will do minor repairs, tune ups or replace some parts—at no cost to you—before transferring your donated bicycle to the Salvation Army. Your final job is to feel good about having helped a disadvantaged person get a usable bicycle.

For more information see web site www.bikeRochester.com and click on the Recycle Cycle logo.

Guided Bike Tours

Rochester Bicycling Club
P.O. Box 10100
Rochester NY 14610
www.rochesterbicyclingclub.com/WordPress/

The Huggers Ski Club, Inc. - Pedal Power
P.O. Box 23921, Rochester, NY 14692-3921
(585) 865-7910
www.huggersskiclub.org/bike.htm

Pack, Paddle, Ski Corp.
P.O. Box 82
S. Lima, NY 14558-0082 USA
(585) 346-5597
www.packpaddleski.com

Cheshire Inn Cycling Tours
6004 Route 21, Naples, NY 14512
(585) 396-2383
www.cheshireinn.com/page9.html

Classic Adventures
P.O. Box 143, Hamlin, NY 14464-0143
bicycling tours in Europe & Erie Canal
(800) 777-8090
(585) 964-8488
www.classicadventures.com

Hidden Trails
Erie Canal Tour
1-888-9-TRAILS
www.hiddentrails.com/outdoor/bike/usa/index.htm

Guided Bike Tours

Parks & Trails New York Parks
Erie Canal Bike Tours
29 Elk Street, Albany, NY 12207
(518) 434-1583
www.ptny.org

Definitions:

Abutment: A structure that supports the end of a bridge.

Aqueduct: A structure that carries a canal across another body of water. The Rochester aqueduct (now Broad Street in downtown), spanned the Genesee River for over 800 feet, and was the largest in the world.

Ballast holds: Heavy material that is placed in the hull of a ship to enhance stability.

Ballast stone: Crushed rock laid to form a bed for roads or railroads.

Blaze orange: A bright, almost fluorescent orange color clothing worn by hunters so they can see each other in the woods.

Causeway: A raised pathway across water or marshland.

CCC: An acronym for Civilian Conservation Corp., a former federal agency of the United States, established in 1933 as part of the New Deal program of President Franklin Delano Roosevelt. The agency was created for the conservation of the country's natural resources and to provide employment for young men during the Great Depression. The CCC enrolled about 3 million unemployed and unmarried men between the ages of 17 and 23 to work on projects including reforestation, construction of fire-observation towers, laying of telephone lines, and development of state parks. Congress voted to abolish the Corps in June 1942.

Change bridge: A bridge over the Erie Canal that allowed mules towing barges and packet boats to reverse directions without having to be unharnessed and transported across the canal.

Culvert: A large tube to allow drainage under a road, embankment, or canal.

DEC: An acronym for Department of Environmental Conservation

Dike: An embankment of earth and rock built to contain water.

Double-track: Two parallel trails created by the depressions made by vehicle tires.

Drumlin: An elongated hill or ridge of glacial drift.

Dual Lock: Locks on the Erie Canal set side by side to allow simultaneous two-way traffic on the canal.

Embankment: A mound of earth or stone built to hold back water or to support a roadway.

Esker: A narrow ridge of land formed when rivers flowed under the glacier in an ice tunnel. Rocky material accumulated on the tunnel beds, and when the glacier melted, a ridge of rubble remained.

Feeder gate: A mechanism that controls water flow from one waterway into another.

Gristmill: A mill for grinding grain into flour.

Guard gate: A large metal partition used as a safeguard when lowered against high water surges, dike leaks, or to lower water for canal repairs.

Hoggee: A mule driver who was paid pitifully low wages to drive mules along the Erie Canal.

Kettles: A pond in a depression created when a large block of ice separated from a glacier. Water running off the glacier deposited gravel and debris all around the ice block. The block melted, leaving behind a rough circular depression.

Mule: The sterile offspring of a male donkey and a female horse.

Packet boat: A long narrow boat used on canals. They provided covered housing for mules and people as well as space to transport cargo.

Recumbent: Lying down. Recumbent bicycles allow the rider to recline backward from a seated position.

Spillway: A channel for an overflow of water, as from a reservoir or canal.

SUNY: An acronym for State University of New York.

Towpath: A path used for towing boats along a canal. The Erie Canal towpath is now the Erie Canalway Trail.

Waste Weir: A dam in a stream or canal used to raise the water level or divert its flow.

Trails Under 5 Miles

Page	Trail Name	Length (miles)
84	North Ponds Park Trail	1.1
170	Hansen Nature Center Trail	1.2
131	Electric Trolley Trail	1.8
189	Big Oak & Bear Cub Loop	1.9
174	Royal Coach Trail	2.2
134	Cartersville - Great Embankment Loop Trail	2.4
191	Fox Run - Racoon Run - Sidewinder Loop	2.6
147	Victor - Lehigh Valley Trail	2.8
192	Stid Hill Multiple Use Area Loop	3.4
80	Webster - Hojack Trail	3.5
178	Canadice Lake Trail	4.0
117	Perinton Hike-Bikeway	4.4
221	Genesee County Park and Forest	4.4
49	Lakeside Beach State Park	4.9
68	Mount Hope Cemetery	any

Trails 5 to 10 Miles

Page	Trail Name	Length (miles)
91	Historic Macedon Erie Canal Route	5.0
37	Hilton Hojack Trail	5.6
1 21	Western Hike-Bikeway to Thomas Creek Wetlands	5.7
96	Canal Park Trailway	5.8
26	Historic Erie Canal and Railroad Loop Trail	6.0
183	Hemlock Lake & Big Oaks Trails	6.0
87	Webster - Route 104 Trail	6.1
192	Stid Hill Multiple Use Area total trails	6.5
107	Hannibal - Hojack Rail Trail	6.6
196	Middlesex Valley Rail Trail	6.8
54	Genesee Valley Park & Genesee Valley Greenway Loop	7.0
61	Genesee River - Downtown Loop Trail	7.0
139	Auburn Trail	6.9
211	Oak Orchard Wildlife Management Area	7.8
110	Howland Island	7.8
45	Hamlin Beach State Park	7.9
163	Ontario Pathways Trail (Stanley to Phelps)	8.7
73	North Genesee River Trail	8.7
68	Mount Hope Cemetery	any

Trails Over 10 Miles

Page	Trail Name	Length (miles)
185	Harriet Hollister Spencer MSRA . . . . .10+	
183	Hemlock Lake & Big Oaks Trails 10.1	
32	Greece Interstate 390 Trail 10.4	
157	Ontario Pathways Trail (Canandaigua to Stanley) . .11.0	
150	Mendon - Lehigh Valley Trail 12.4	
216	Iroquois National Wildlife Refuge and Tonawanda Wildlife Management Area 12.5	
101	Fair Haven - Cato Trail (Cayuga County Trail) 13.0	
41	Hamlin Hojack Trail 14.0	
68	Mount Hope Cemetery 14.5	
231	Erie Canalway Trail (Palmyra to Pittsford) 18.0	
240	Erie Canalway Trail (Pittsford to Spencerport) 19.1	
247	Erie Canalway Trail (Spencerport to Albion) 22.2	
202	Genesee Valley Greenway (Chili to Cuylerville) 25.6	
254	Erie Canalway Trail (Albion to Lockport) 28.0	

Combination Trails (the long stuff)

Page	Trail Name	Combined Length (miles)
54	Genesee Valley Park & Genesee Valley Greenway Loop	
61	Genesee River - Downtown Loop Trail 14.0	
54	Genesee Valley Park & Genesee Valley Greenway Loop .	
240	Erie Canalway Trail 94.3	
61	Genesee River - Downtown Loop Trail	
240	Erie Canalway Trail 94.3	
80	Webster - Hojack Trail	
84	North Ponds Park Trail	
87	Webster - Route 104 Trail .10.7	
101	Fair Haven - Cato Trail	
107	Hannibal - Hojack Rail Trail 19.6	
139	Auburn Trail	
147	Victor - Lehigh Valley Trail	
150	Mendon- Lehigh Valley Trail 22.7	
147	Victor - Lehigh Valley Trail	
150	Mendon- Lehigh Valley Trail 5.2	

	Erie Canalway Trail (Newark to Palmyra)	
231	Erie Canalway Trail (Palmyra to Pittsford)	
240	Erie Canalway Trail (Pittsford to Spencerport)	
247	Erie Canalway Trail (Spencerport to Albion)	
254	Erie Canalway Trail (Albion to Lockport) 96.8

| 121 | Western Hike-Bikeway to Thomas Creek Wetlands | |
| 231 | Erie Canalway Trail . . . . .93.0 |

| 126 | Historic Erie Canal and Railroad Loop Trail | |
| 231 | Erie Canalway Trail . . . . .93.3 |

| 131 | Electric Trolley Trail | |
| 231 | Erie Canalway Trail . . . . .89.1 |

| 157 | Ontario Pathways Trail (Canandaigua to Stanley) | |
| 163 | Ontario Pathways Trail (Stanley to Phelps) . . . . .19.7 |

| 54 | Genesee Valley Park & Genesee Valley Greenway Loop | |
| 202 | Genesee Valley Greenway (Chili to Cuylerville) . . . . .32.6 |

231	Erie Canalway Trail	
54	Genesee Valley Park & Genesee Valley Greenway Loop	
202	Genesee Valley Greenway (Chili to Cuylerville) 119.9

Loop Trails

Page	Trail Name	Length (miles)
45	Hamlin Beach State Park	7.9
49	Lakeside Beach State Park	4.9
54	Genesee Valley Park & Genesee Valley Greenway Loop	7.0
61	Genesee River - Downtown Loop Trail	7.0
68	Mount Hope Cemetery	any
84	North Ponds Park Trail	1.1
91	Historic Macedon Erie Canal Route	5.0
110	Howland Island	7.8
126	Historic Erie Canal and Railroad Loop Trail	6.0
131	Electric Trolley Trail	1.8
134	Cartersville - Great Embankment Loop Trail	2.4
170	Hansen Nature Center Trail	1.2
174	Royal Coach Trail	2.2
178	Canadice Lake Trail	4.0
183	Hemlock Lake & Big Oaks Trails	10.1
185	Harriet Hollister Spencer MSRA	10+
189	Big Oak & Bear Cub Loop	1.9
191	Fox Run - Racoon Run - Sidewinder Loop	2.6
192	Stid Hill Multiple Use Area Loop	3.4
211	Oak Orchard Wildlife Management Area	7.8
216	Iroquois National Wildlife Refuge and Tonawanda Wildlife Management Area	12.5
221	Genesee County Park and Forest	4.4

Easy Trails

Page	Trail Name	Length (miles)
32	Greece Interstate 390 Trail	10.4
37	Hilton Hojack Trail	5.6
41	Hamlin Hojack Trail	14.0
45	Hamlin Beach State Park	7.9
61	Genesee River - Downtown Loop Trail	7.0
84	North Ponds Park Trail	1.1
87	Webster - Route 104 Trail	6.1
91	Historic Macedon Erie Canal Route	5.0
101	Fair Haven - Cato Trail (Cayuga County Trail)	13.0
107	Hannibal - Hojack Rail Trail	6.6
116	Perinton Hike-Bikeway	4.4
131	Electric Trolley Trail	1.8
139	Auburn Trail	6.9
147	Victor - Lehigh Valley Trail	2.8
150	Mendon - Lehigh Valley Trail	12.4
157	Ontario Pathways Trail (Canandaigua to Stanley)	11.0
163	Ontario Pathways Trail (Stanley to Phelps)	8.7
170	Hansen Nature Center Trail	1.2
178	Canadice Lake Trail	4.0
183	Hemlock Lake & Big Oaks Trails	10.1
216	Iroquois National Wildlife Refuge and Tonawanda Wildlife Management Area	12.5
231	Erie Canalway Trail (Palmyra to Pittsford)	18.0
240	Erie Canalway Trail (Pittsford to Spencerport)	19.1
247	Erie Canalway Trail (Spencerport to Albion)	22.2
254	Erie Canalway Trail (Albion to Lockport)	28.0

Moderate Trails

Page	Trail Name	Length (miles)
49	Lakeside Beach State Park	4.9
54	Genesee Valley Park & Genesee Valley Greenway Loop	7.0
68	Mount Hope Cemetery	14.5
73	North Genesee River Trail	8.7
80	Webster - Hojack Trail	3.5

96	Canal Park Trailway	.5.8
121	Western Hike-Bikeway to Thomas Creek Wetlands	.5.7
126	Historic Erie Canal and Railroad Loop Trail	.6.0
134	Cartersville - Great Embankment Loop Trail	.2.4
183	Hemlock Lake & Big Oaks Trails	.10.1
185	Harriet Hollister Spencer MSRA	.10+
189	Big Oak & Bear Cub Loop	.1.9
191	Fox Run - Racoon Run - Sidewinder Loop	.2.6
196	Middlesex Valley Rail Trail	.6.8
202	Genesee Valley Greenway (Chili to Cuylerville)	.25.6
211	Oak Orchard Wildlife Management Area	.7.8

Difficult Trails

Page	Trail Name	Length (miles)
110	Howland Island	.7.8
174	Royal Coach Trail	.2.2
192	Stid Hill Multiple Use Area	.3.3
221	Genesee County Park and Forest	.4.4

Mountain Biking Trails

Page	Trail Name	Length (miles)
73	North Genesee River Trail	.8.7
174	Royal Coach Trail	.2.2
178	Canadice Lake Trail	.4.0
185	Harriet Hollister Spencer MSRA	.10+
189	Big Oak & Bear Cub Loop	.1.9
191	Fox Run - Racoon Run - Sidewinder Loop	.2.6
192	Stid Hill Multiple Use Area Loop	.3.4
192	Stid Hill Multiple Use Area total trails	.6.5

Camping Nearby

Page	Trail Name	Length (miles)
45	Hamlin Beach State Park	7.9
49	Lakeside Beach State Park	4.9
101	Fair Haven - Cato Trail (Cayuga County Trail)	13.0
110	Howland Island	7.8
231	Erie Canalway Trail (Palmyra to Pittsford)	18.0
247	Erie Canalway Trail (Spencerport to Albion)	22.2

Swimming Nearby

Page	Trail Name	Length (miles)
45	Hamlin Beach State Park	7.9
84	North Ponds Park Trail	1.1
101	Fair Haven - Cato Trail (Cayuga County Trail)	13.0
202	Genesee Valley Greenway (Chili to Cuylerville)	25.6

Paved Trails

Page	Trail Name	Length (miles)
32	Greece Interstate 390 Trail	10.4
45	Hamlin Beach State Park	7.9
54	Genesee Valley Park & Genesee Valley Greenway Loop	7.0
61	Genesee River - Downtown Loop Trail	7.0
68	Mount Hope Cemetery	14.5
84	North Ponds Park Trail	1.1
87	Webster - Route 104 Trail	6.1
231	Erie Canalway Trail (Fairport Area)	3.5
240	Erie Canalway Trail (Pittsford to Greece)	13.3

Word Index

104 Trail: 87-90
10-speed bikes: 23-24
390 Trail: 32-36

A

Adams, William: 250
Adam's Basin B&B: 249-250
Adopt-a-trail: 252
Aldrich change bridge: 230, 233-234
Aldrich family: 171
Anthony, Susan B.: 71
Aqueduct: 233-234, 242, 268
Auburn Trail: 139-146

B

Ballast: 268
Ballooners: 23-24
Barge Canal: 93, 98, 111, 229, 242
Barry, Patrick: 71
Bausch, John Jacob: 71
Bed &Breakfasts:
   Canal Country Inn: 259-260
   Country Cottage B&B: 260
   Friendship Manor B&B: 256
   Gables of Palmyra: 234
   Garden View B&B: 258-259
   Hambleton House B&B: 262
   Liberty House B&B: 234
   Oliver Loud's Country Inn: 119, 238-239
   Portico B&B: 251
   Rosewood B&B: 252
   Twenty Woodlawn B&B: 236
   Victorian B&B: 251
Berlin Lock: 100
Bicycle Outfitters: 251
Big Oak & Bear Cub Loop: 189
Bike clubs: 263-264
Bike Racks: 29-30
Bike Shops:
   Bicycle Outfitters: 251
   Bike Zone, The: 35-36
   Park Avenue Bike Shop: 128, 160
   RV&E Bike & Skate: 236
   Sugar's Bike Shop: 249
   Towpath Bike Shop: 128, 133, 239
Bike Zone, The: 35-36
Black Diamond: 148, 152-153
Blaze orange: 12, 112, 189, 199, 214, 218, 268
Blazes: 15
Blog: 3, 283
BMX: 23-24

Boat Tours:
   Colonial Belle: 236
   Lockport Cave & Underground Boat Ride: 261
   Lockport Locks & Canal Tours: 261
   MidLakes Navigation Company: 261
   Rentals of canoes, kayaks, bikes: 64-66, 76,
      237, 238, 251
   Sam Patch: 64-66, 238, 239
Bookhug Book Holder: 286
Braille trail: 223-224
Britt, Jim: 9
Bushnell, William: 237

C

Calories: 11
Calvin, Todd: 9
Camping: 46, 50, 103, 113, 235, 252, 276
Canadice Lake Trail: 178-182
Canal Country Inn: 259-260
Canal Park Trailway: 96-100
Canandaigua Corning Line: 159
Canoe: 64-66, 76, 237, 238, 251
Cartersville: 135, 138
Cartersville-Great Embankment Loop Trail: 134-138
Carthage: 76
Castletown: 64, 74
Cayuga County Planning Board: 10, 102, 107
CCC: 47, 111, 268
Celerifere: 20
Cement: 75-77
Center Park: 119-120
Change bridge: 233-234
Charlotte: 76
Chase Farms: 120
Cheshire Inn Cycling Tours: 266
Children: 26
City of Rochester, Bureau of Parks and Recreation:
   10, 62-64, 74
City of Rochester, Water and Lighting Bureau: 10,
   179, 184
Civilian Conservation Corp: 47, 111, 268
Classic Adventures: 266
Clinton's Ditch: 93-95, 97-100, 127, 228, 237, 245
Clothing: 28
Coal: 148, 152
Coaster-brake bikes: 23-24
Cobblestone: 141-144, 171
Cobblestone Museum: 256
Colonial Belle: 236
Comfort bikes: 24
Consolidated Rail Corporation: 75

Country Cottage B&B: 260
Coventry Sewing Machine Company: 21
Crescent Trail Association: 9
Cruisers: 23-24
Culvert Road: 257-258
Cushing, Pat & Don: 58
Cyclotour Guide Books: 264

D
DaVinci, Leonardo: 20
Davis, Bill: 76
DEC (Department of Environmental
    Conservation): 10, 110, 268
Derailleur: 23-24
DeSivrac: 20
Despatch: 118
Difficult: 14
Disc golf: 33-36
Dockmaster building: 118
Dogs: 27
Domina, Susan: 10
Donate bikes: 265
Double-track: 268
Douglass, Frederick: 71
Drinking water: 179-180, 185
Drumlins: 103, 112
Dry dock: 262
Dumpling Hill Lock: 207, 208
Dunlop tires: 21
Dykstra, Bill: 10

E
Easy: 14
Egypt Park: 117-120
Electric Trolley Trail: 131-133
Ellwanger, George: 71
Erie Canal: 56-59, 64, 91-95, 97-100, 111, 127-
    130, 134-138, 228-262
Erie Canalway Trail - Albion to Lockport: 254-262
Erie Canalway Trail - Palmyra to Pittsford: 231-239
Erie Canalway Trail - Pittsford to Spencerport:
    240-246
Erie Canalway Trail - Spencerport to Albion: 247-253
Esker: 70, 135
Essroc Materials, Inc.: 75-76
Ewers, Todd: 189
Exercise trail: 33-36
Ezine/Blog: 3, 283

F
Fair Haven - Cato Trail: 101-106

Fair Haven Beach State Park: 103, 108
Fairport, Village of: 123
Famous Five locks: 261
Farr, Jim: 10
Feeder gate: 207
Flood: 136, 138
Footprint Press Guidebooks: 264, 284-285
Fox Run-Racoon Run-Sidewinder Loop: 191
Frankfort: 76
Friends of Genesee Valley Greenway: 205, 208
Friends of Mount Hope Cemetery: 72
Friendship Manor B&B: 256
Freeman, Rich & Sue: 282-283

G
Gables of Palmyra: 234
Gage, Kyle: 9
Ganondagan National Historic Site: 145
Garden View B&B: 258-259
Genesee County Park and Forest: 221-226
Genesee Region Trails Coalition: 9
Genesee River: 73-78
Genesee River - Downtown Loop Trail: 61-67
Genesee Riverway: 74-75
Genesee Transportation Council: 9
Genesee Valley Canal: 64, 205, 207
Genesee Valley Cycling Club: 263
Genesee Valley Greenway: 54-60, 202-210
Genesee Valley Greenway, Friends of: 9, 55
Genesee Valley Park: 54-60, 61-67
Genesee Valley Park & Genesee Valley Greenway
    Loop: 54-60
George Bridge: 206, 209
Gillespie, Frank A.: 72
Gould, General Jacob: 71
Granger, John: 159
Great Embankment: 135-138, 237-238
GREATS: 263
Greece Interstate 390 Trail: 32-36
Greece, Town of: 10, 33
Guard gate: 268
Guided Bike Tours: 266-267

H
Hambleton House B&B: 262
Hamlin Beach State Park: 10, 45-48
Hamlin Hojack Trail: 41-44
Hanford's Mill: 78
Hannibal - Hojack Rail Trail: 101, 107-109
Hansen Nature Center: 9, 27
Hansen Nature Center Trail: 170-173

Word Index

Harriet Hollister Spencer Memorial State
  Recreation Area: 187-191
Hartwell's Basin: 237
Helmet: 25, 26
Hemlock Lake & Big Oaks Trails: 183-186
Henrietta Parks Department: 10, 152
Henry, Peter S.: 9
Heron rookery: 198
Hilton Hojack Trail: 37-40
Historic Erie Canal and Railroad Loop Trail: 126-130
Historic Macedon Erie Canal Route: 91-95
Hobby Horse: 20
Hoggee: 269
Hojack Railroad: 37-40, 41-44, 80-83, 107-109
Holley, Myron: 251
Holy Sepulchre Cemetery: 75, 77
Howe, Karen: 10
Howland Island: 110-114
Huggers Ski Club: 263, 266
Hunting: 12, 112, 189, 199, 214, 218
Hurricane Agnes: 159-160
Hybrid bikes: 24

I

Ice cream: 120, 124, 128, 133, 209, 236, 237,
  238, 239, 242, 244, 249, 259
Indians: 64, 70, 200, 206, 210, 239
Ira Corners: 105-106
Irondequoit Flats: 76, 78
Iroquois National Wildlife Refuge and Tonawanda
  Wildlife Management Area: 216-220

J

Junction Lock: 245

K

Kaufman, Nick: 22
Kayak: 64-66, 237, 238, 251
Kettle: 69-70
King's Landing: 76, 77

L

Lake Ontario Shore Railroad: 38, 82
Lakeside Beach State Park: 10, 49-52
Landmark Society of Rochester: 72
Lehigh Valley Railroad: 101-106, 147-149, 150-
  156, 196-200
Liberty House B&B: 234
Lincoln, President Abraham: 159
Lock, Berlin: 100

Lock 2: 207
Lock 5: 207, 209
Lock 30: 93-95, 235
Lock 32: 126-130, 242-243
Lock 33: 242-243
Locks 34 & 35: 260-261
Lock 60: 93-94, 235
Lock 60 Locktenders Association: 92
Lock 61: 93-94
Lock 62: 128, 129
Lock 71: 93
Lockport Cave & Underground Boat Ride: 261
Lockport Locks & Canal Tours: 261
Lollypop Farm: 118-120
Lomb, Henry: 71
Lower Falls: 76

M

Macedon Trails Committee: 9, 92
Macedon, Town of: 92
MacMillan, Kirkpatrick: 20
Markers: 15
Massauga Bike Tours: 266
McCormick reapers: 250
McCrackenville: 76
Mendon - Lehigh Valley Trail: 150-156
Mendon Foundation, The: 9, 152
Michaux, Ernest: 21
Michaux, Pierre: 21
Middlesex Valley Rail Trail: 196-200
Middlesex Valley Railroad: 198-199
MidLakes Navigation Company: 261
Moderate: 14
Monroe County Parks Department: 10, 55, 74, 152
Moondance Pet Boarding: 10
Morgan, Joseph: 208
Mormon: 233
Mount Hope Cemetery: 27, 68-72
Mountain bikes: 23-24, 275
Mule: 269
Museum: 22, 152, 171, 249, 252, 256, 258, 261, 262

N

National Mountain Bike Patrol: 194
Native Americans: 64, 70, 200, 206, 210, 239
Newark (Erie Canalway Trail): 228, 230
New York Central Railroad: 128, 141, 159, 235
New York Parks & Conservation Association: 252, 267
New York State Canal Corporation: 10, 64, 124,
  228, 252
New York State Department of Environmental

Conservation: 10, 110, 193, 197, 205, 208, 212, 217
New York State Office of Parks, Recreation and Historic Preservation: 188, 208
Nielson, Waldo J.: 67, 243
North Genesee River Trail: 73-78
North Ponds Park Trail: 84-86
Northern Central: 159
No-trace ethics: 19

O

Oak Orchard Wildlife Management Area: 211-215
Oak trees: 207-208
Odenbach Shipyard: 127, 129
Oliver Loud's Country Inn: 119, 238-239
Olmsted, Frederick Law: 56, 243
Ontario Pathways: 9, 159, 166
Ontario Pathways Trail: 157-162, 163-168
Orchard View B&B: 256
O'Rorke bridge: 76-77
O'Rorke, Colonel Patrick: 76

P

Pack, Paddle, Ski Corp.: 266
Park Avenue Bike Shop: 128, 160
Paved trails: 276
Pedal Power: 263, 266
Pedaling History Museum: 22
Penfield Trails Committee: 9
Penn Central Corporation: 159-160
Pennsylvania Railroad: 207
Perinton Hike-Bikeway: 116-120, 121-125
Perinton, Town of: 117
Phelps, Oliver III: 159
Pittsford Parks and Recreation:10, 127, 132, 135, 175
Pneumatic tube: 21
Poor House Farm: 223
Portico B&B: 251
Prisoner of war camp: 112
Pullman, George: 256
Pump house: 141-144
Purple loosestrife: 213-214

Q

Queen Victoria: 70-71

R

Racks: 29-30
Railroads:
    Canandaigua Corning Line: 159
    Consolidated Rail Corporation: 75

Hojack Railroad: 37-40, 41-44, 80-83, 107-109
Lake Ontario Shore Railroad: 38, 82
Lehigh Valley Railroad: 101-106, 147-149, 150-156, 196-200
Middlesex Valley Railroad: 198-199
New York Central Railroad: 128, 141, 159, 235
Northern Central: 159
Penn Central Corporation: 159-160
Pennsylvania Railroad: 207
Rochester and Auburn Railroad: 128-129, 141
Rochester and Eastern Rapid Railway: 132, 141, 237-238
Rochester and Southern Railroad: 66, 244
Rochester, Syracuse and Eastern Rapid Railway: 117-118, 124, 236
Rome, Watertown and Ogdensburg Railroad 82
RARE: 263
RATS: 263
Reapers: 250
Recumbent club: 263
Recycle Cycle Program: 265
Reisem, Richard O.: 72
Renaissance Festival: 103, 108
Rentals of canoes, kayaks, bikes: 64-66, 76, 237, 238, 251
Richardson's Canal Inn: 237-238
Riverside Cemetery: 73-78
Rochester and Auburn Railroad: 128-129, 141
Rochester and Eastern Rapid Railway: 132, 141, 237-238
Rochester and Southern Railroad: 66, 244
Rochester Bicycling Club: 9, 21, 193, 194, 263, 266
Rochester Junction: 152, 154
Rochester Running Track: 75
Rochester, Bureau of Parks and Recreation: 10, 62-64, 74
Rochester, Colonel Nathaniel: 71
Rochester, Syracuse and Eastern Rapid Railway: 117-118, 124, 236
Rochester, Water and Lighting Bureau: 10, 179, 184
Rochesterville: 64, 76, 242
Rome, Watertown and Ogdensburg Railroad: 82
Root, Don: 10
Rosewood B&B: 252
Rowland, Thomas J.: 10
Royal Coach Trail: 174-177
RV&E Bike & Skate: 236

S

Salvation Army: 265

Word Index

Sam Patch: 64-66, 238, 239
Seneca Park: 73-78
Seneca Trail: 145
Sibley, Hiram: 71
Sibley, John: 159
Sidepath Association: 21
Signs: 15
Slusarczyk, James: 10
Smith, Joseph: 233
Spencer, Daniel: 248
Stagecoach stop: 119
Starley Rover: 21
Starley, James: 21
Stid Hill Multiple Use Area: 192-195
Stone Street Trail: 95
Stone, Simon: 136
Strong, Margaret Woodbury: 71
Stutson Street bridge: 76
Sugar's Bike Shop: 249
Swift, John: 233
Swimming: 46, 85, 103, 206, 209, 276

T

Tandem club: 263
Terry bicycles: 22, 264
Terry, Georgena: 22
Thomas Creek Wetlands: 122-125, 236
Thompson, R. W.: 21
Tinker Homestead Museum: 171
Tinker Nature Park: 170-173
Tonawanda Wildlife Management Area: 216-220
Towpath Bike Shop: 128, 133, 239
Trailer: 26, 29-30
Train station: 64, 66, 141, 145, 148, 152
Triathletes club: 263
Trolley: 117-118, 124, 132-133, 141, 237-238
Turning Point Park: 73-78
Twenty Woodlawn B&B: 236

U

University of Rochester: 61-67

V

Vaeth, John: 2
Vanderbilt, Corenlius: 141
Velocipede: 21
Victor - Lehigh Valley Trail: 139, 147-149
Victor Hiking Trails: 9, 141, 147
Victorian B&B: 251
Von Drais, Baron Karl: 20

W

Wadsworth Junction: 209
Walnut Hill Farms: 175
Waste weir: 100, 251, 256, 259, 269
Water: 28, 239
Water supply: 179-180
Water Tower: 165, 167
Waterfall: 76, 252, 257, 259
Wayne County Planning Department: 10, 97
Webster - Hojack Trail: 80-83
Webster - Route 104 Trail: 87-90
Webster Parks and Recreation Department: 10, 85
Webster Trails, Friends of: 9, 81-83
Webster, Town of: 10, 88
Western Hike-Bikeway to Thomas Creek
    Wetlands: 121-125
Western NY Mountain Biking Association: 264
Wilson, Jared: 159
Wilson, William: 71
Women's bicycles: 264

Y

York Landing: 210

About the Authors

The authors, Rich and Sue Freeman, decided to make their living from what they love—being outdoors. In 1996 they left corporate jobs to spend six months hiking 2,200 miles on the Appalachian Trail from Georgia to Maine. That adventure deepened their love of the outdoors and inspired them to share this love by introducing others to the joys of hiking. Since most people don't have the option (let alone the desire) to undertake a six-month trek, they decided to focus on short hikes, near home. The result was the first version of *Take A Hike! Family Walks in the Rochester Area.* They went on to explore hiking, bicycling, skiing, snowshoeing, water-falling, and paddling trails throughout Central and Western New York State. They have written 14 guidebooks.

The Freemans' passion for outdoor adventure continues. In 1997 they thru-hiked the 500-mile long Bruce Trail in Ontario, Canada. In 1998 they bicycled across New York State, following the Erie Canalway Trail and 1999 found them hiking a segment of the Florida Trail. In 2000 they bicycled the C&O Canal Trail from Washington D.C to Cumberland, MD. In 2001 they hiked across northern Spain on the Camino de Santiago Trail and hiked a section of the International Appalachian Trail in Quebec, Canada. In 2002 They climbed the highest mountain in Africa—Mt. Kilimanjaro. They hiked across England on the Coast to Coast trail in 2003. They returned to Africa in 2006 to hike the countryside and climb an active volcano.

The Freemans publish a free Blog on outdoor recreation in Central and Western New York State, called *New York Outdoors*. Find it on the home page at www.footprintpress.com, or go directly to:

http://newyorkoutdoors.wordpress.com

Since beginning their new career writing and publishing books, the Freemans have pared down their living expenses and are enjoying a simpler lifestyle. They now have control of their own destiny and the freedom to head into the woods for a refreshing respite when the urge strikes. Still, their life is infinitely more cluttered than when they carried all their worldly needs on their backs for six months on the Appalachian Trail.

Hiking:

Peak Experiences–Hiking the Highest Summits in NY, County by County
ISBN# 0-9656974-01   U.S. $16.95
A guide to the highest point in each county of New York State.

Take A Hike! Family Walks in the Rochester Area (second edition)
ISBN# 0-9656974-79   U.S. $16.95
60 day hikes within a 15-mile radius of Rochester, N.Y.

Take A Hike! Family Walks in New York's Finger Lakes Region
ISBN# 1-930480-20-2   U.S. $19.95
68 day hike trails throughout the Finger Lakes Region.

Bruce Trail – An Adventure Along the Niagara Escarpment
ISBN# 0-9656974-36   U.S. $16.95
Learn the secrets of long-distance backpackers on a five-week hike
in Ontario, Canada, as they explore the abandoned Welland
Canal routes, caves, ancient cedar forests, and white cobblestone
beaches along Georgian Bay.

Backpacking Trails of Central & Western New York State   U.S. $2.00
A 10 page booklet on the backpackable trails of central and western
NY with contact information to obtain maps and trail guides.

Canoeing & Kayaking:

Take a Paddle - Western New York Quiet Water for Canoes & Kayaks
ISBN# 1-930480-23-7   U.S. $18.95
Offering over 250 miles of flat-water creeks and rivers, and 20
ponds and lakes, this guide provides a fun way to explore
Western New York.

Take a Paddle - Finger Lakes New York Quiet Water for Canoes & Kayaks
ISBN# 1-930480-24-5   U.S. $18.95
Offering over 370 miles of flat-water creeks and rivers, and 35
ponds and lakes, this guide provides a fun way to explore the
beautiful Finger Lakes region.

Cross-country Skiing and Snowshoeing:

Snow Trails–Cross-country Ski and Snowshoe in Central and Western NY
ISBN# 0-9656974-52   U.S. $16.95
80 mapped locations for winter fun on skis or snowshoes.

Bird Watching:

Birding in Central & Western New York
Best Trails & Water Routes for Finding Birds
ISBN# 1-930480-00-8   U.S. $16.95
70 of the best places to spot birds on foot, from a car, or from a canoe.

Bicycling:

Take Your Bike! Family Rides in the Rochester Area (second edition)
ISBN# 1-930480-02-4   U.S. $18.95
Rail trails, paved bike paths and woods trails, combine to create 42 bicycle adventures within an easy drive of Rochester, NY.

Take Your Bike! Family Rides in the Finger Lakes & Genesee Valley Region
ISBN# 0-9656974-44   U.S. $16.95
Rail trails, woods trails, and little-used country roads combine to create 40 bicycle adventures through central and western NY.

Take Your Bike! Family Rides in New York's Finger Lakes Region
ISBN# 1-930480-22-9   U.S. $19.95
43 bicycle adventures in the Finger Lakes Region, range from paved rail-trails to rugged mountain biking trails.

Waterfall Fun:

200 Waterfalls in Central and Western New York – A Finders' Guide
ISBN# 1-930480-00-8   U.S. $18.95
Explore the many diverse waterfalls that dot the creeks and gorges of central and western New York State.

Explore History:

Cobblestone Quest - Road Tours of New York's Historic Buildings
ISBN# 1-930480-19-9   U.S. $19.95
17 self-guided tours for observing the history and diversity of unique cobblestone buildings built before the Civil War. Enjoy the tours by car, motorcycle or bicycle.

For details, sample maps and chapters explore web site:

www.footprintpress.com

Bookhug
the hands-free open book holder

If you're reading a book and you find yourself thinking that two hands are simply not enough, the Bookhug is the answer to your dilemma. The Bookhug was designed to hold hard and soft cover books open and upright, leaving the reader's hands completely free.

Its unique, one-piece design accommodates most books up to 1.5" thick. It will conveniently hold a paperback while you eat, an instruction manual while you work, a cookbook while you cook, or a textbook while you type at the computer.

* A convenient and simple holder for large and small books.
* Attractive, compact, unbreakable.
* Packaged in an attractive gift box.

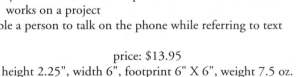

Bookhug will:
* hold cookbooks in the kitchen
* enable reader to study or write
* permit leisure reading while eating
* hold text or copy when typing
* display how-to books while a person
    works on a project
* enable a person to talk on the phone while referring to text

price: $13.95
height 2.25", width 6", footprint 6" X 6", weight 7.5 oz.
durable steel with a shiny black/silver finish

Order yours today at
www.displaystands4you.com

Yes, I'd like to order Footprint Press books:

#		price/book
_____	200 Waterfalls in Central & Western NY	$18.95
_____	Peak Experiences—Hiking the Highest Summits in NY	$16.95
_____	NYS County Summit Club patch	$2.00
_____	Snow Trails—Cross-country Ski & Snowshoe	$16.95
_____	Birdng in Central & Western NY	$16.95
_____	Take A Paddle - Western NY	$18.95
_____	Take A Paddle - Finger Lakes NY	$18.95
_____	Cobblestone Quest	$19.95
_____	Take A Hike! Family Walks in the Rochester Area	$16.95
_____	Take A Hike! Family Walks in NY's Finger Lakes	$19.95
_____	Take Your Bike! Family Rides in the Rochester Area	$18.95
_____	Take Your Bike! Family Rides in the Genesee Valley	$16.95
_____	Take Your Bike! Family Rides in NY's Finger Lakes	$19.95
_____	Bruce Trail—An Adventure Along the Niagara Escarpment	$16.95
_____	Backpacking Trails of Central & Western NYS	$2.00
_____	Alter—A Simple Path to Emotional Wellness	$16.95
_____	Bookhug hands-free book holder	$13.95

Sub-total $_____

FL state and Canadian residents add 7% tax $_____

Shipping & Handling $3.50

Total enclosed: $_____

Your Name: _____

Address: _____

City: _____ State (Province): _____

Zip (Postal Code): _____ Country: _____

Make check payable and mail to:
Footprint Press, Inc.
303 Pine Glen Court, Englewood, FL 34223

Or order through web site **www.footprintpress.com**

Footprint Press books are available at special discounts when purchased in bulk for sales
promotions, premiums, or fund raising. Call (941) 474-8316.